DATA MANAGEMENT ESSENTIALS USING SAS AND JMP

SAS programming is a creative and iterative process designed to empower you to make the most of your organization's data. This friendly guide provides you with a repertoire of essential SAS tools for data management, whether you're a new or an infrequent user. Most useful to students and programmers with little or no SAS experience, it takes a no-frills, hands-on tutorial approach to getting started with the software.

You'll find immediate guidance in navigating, exploring, visualizing, cleaning, formatting, and reporting on data using SAS and JMP. Step-by-step demonstrations, screenshots, handy tips, and practical exercises with solutions equip you to explore, interpret, process, and summarize data independently, efficiently, and effectively.

Julie Kezik is a biostatistician at the Yale Center for Perinatal, Pediatric, and Environmental Epidemiology. Her primary research interests are assessing the effects of indoor and outdoor air pollution on at-risk populations, and she currently focuses on providing statistical analysis and research support for epidemiological studies of environmental exposures and early childhood health outcomes. Kezik's current work uses a combination of measured data, traffic information, and health outcomes to help create interventions that will improve health.

Melissa Hill is a clinical programmer at Cd3 Inc. where she uses SAS to perform and support the design and programming of clinical data structures related to drug development. Prior to her position at Cd3 Inc., she worked as an epidemiologist at the Yale Center for Perinatal, Pediatric, and Environmental Epidemiology. During that time, Hill used SAS to support her various roles at the CPPEE including programmer analyst, field study coordinator, and research associate. She enjoys sharing her diverse SAS experience with other members of her team and developing new ways to harness the broad range of tools that SAS provides.

Data Management Essentials Using SAS and JMP

Julie Kezik, MS

Melissa Hill, MPH

CAMBRIDGE
UNIVERSITY PRESS

CAMBRIDGE
UNIVERSITY PRESS

One Liberty Plaza, 20th Floor, New York, NY 10006, USA

Cambridge University Press is part of the University of Cambridge.

It furthers the University's mission by disseminating knowledge in the pursuit of education, learning, and research at the highest international levels of excellence.

www.cambridge.org
Information on this title: www.cambridge.org/9781107535039

First published 2016

Printed in the United States of America by Sheridan Books, Inc.

A catalog record for this publication is available from the British Library.

Library of Congress Cataloging in Publication Data
Names: Kezik, Julie, 1982– author. | Hill, Melissa E., 1982– author.
Title: Data management essentials using SAS and JMP / Julie Kezik, Yale
School of Public Health, Melissa Hill, Yale University Center for Perinatal Pediatric and
Environmental Epidemiology.
Description: New York : Cambridge University Press, 2016. | Includes bibliographical references.
Identifiers: LCCN 2015043490
Subjects: LCSH: Database management. | Data structures (Computer science) | SAS (Computer file) |
JMP (Computer file)
Classification: LCC QA76.9.D3 K358984 2016 | DDC 005.74–dc23
LC record available at http://lccn.loc.gov/2015043490

ISBN 978-1-107-11456-2 Hardback
ISBN 978-1-107-53503-9 Paperback

Contents

Acknowledgments

We would like to thank our friends and colleagues at the Yale University Center for Perinatal, Pediatric, and Environmental Epidemiology for their support and encouragement.

Another very special expression of gratitude to our families for countless hours of childcare.

About This Book

In research groups around the world, SAS is used not only by statisticians and investigators for data analysis but by programmers and data managers to handle seemingly endless libraries of priceless data. These data management teams often include support staff who have been selected and hired for their attention to detail and patience with meticulous tasks, but who are not necessarily fluent in SAS. The typical solution is for more advanced users to do excessive and simplistic programming to provide the output necessary for whatever task the assistant will be handling. This cycle creates extra work for advanced users and limits the independent effectiveness of the support team – a frustrating arrangement for all parties involved.

In the face of this conundrum we sought a training program for our support team. We found that no training program existed that met our specific needs; available resources were either too costly, too time consuming, or too statistically driven. Eventually we developed and initiated our own basic SAS training program for our programming and research assistants. Spending some structured time with employees while they explored SAS was the most economical way to teach basic users the skills they needed to complete daily tasks. Since training our own staff, we have experienced increased productivity by an empowered support team. This book is a result of that successful endeavour, which inspired us to share our curriculum with other groups who are undoubtedly faced with the same challenge.

SAS programming is a creative and iterative process designed to empower the user. The purpose of this text is not to instruct users on how to complete specific tasks, but to provide a toolkit of essentials for new and infrequent users. When used appropriately, this book will enable these users to explore, interpret, process, and summarize data independently.

How to Use This Book

This book can be used from cover to cover as a hands-on training manual or simply as a desk reference. The content is directed at first-time or infrequent users who seek immediate applicability in order to navigate, clean, and report data. In an effort to truly teach the most basic SAS skills essential to data management, this text uses a multitude of examples and screenshots to walk the reader through step-by-step instructions for executing commonly used techniques and procedures. Beginning with Chapter 2, there is a 'Test Your Skills' section with practice tasks and full solution sets. You will find that in SAS there is more than one way to accomplish many of the tasks; the solutions provided should in no way be perceived as exhaustive. All of the examples and practice tasks are based on datasets found in the sashelp library or created by you, the user, and require no additional software or downloading. The versions of software used for examples include SAS 9.4, SAS Enterprise Guide 4.3, and JMP Pro 10.

CHAPTER 1

Navigation

Working in SAS puts a cornucopia of resources literally at our fingertips; a thorough tour of the nooks and crannies of this dynamic software will promote efficient navigation of the product and help us identify the tools that are best suited to any given task. In this chapter we begin with a guided tour of the five Base SAS windows, exploring their purpose and utility from the programmer's perspective. We then further explore those windows in the context of data migration. Finally, we touch upon SAS Enterprise Guide – comparing it with the SAS Windowing Environment and describing how the user can benefit from working in Enterprise Guide.

SAS WINDOWING ENVIRONMENT

To begin our tour of the SAS Windows, let's open the application. A toolbar can easily be identified near the top of the screen (Figure 1.1) as well as two main work spaces (Figure 1.2a).

Figure 1.1 shows the standard SAS drop-down menus and toolbar. The File and Edit menu include common commands such as new, open, save, print, copy, and paste. File and Edit menu tasks can also be executed from the toolbar using standard icons. The View and Run menus are more unique to SAS. The View menu contains a list of SAS windows and folders; it allows instant

Running Person

FIGURE 1.1. SAS Toolbar.

access to these windows (an important piece of information to remember should you accidentally close a window). Run allows the user to submit syntax. The more customary method for submitting programs is the Run icon, also known as the running person, which appears on the SAS toolbar.

Figure 1.2a includes the Editor, Log, and Output window tabs (bottom right-hand side of the screen). The Editor is where syntax (also referred to as code) is written; this is the way the programmer communicates with SAS software. Executing code is the primary way to accomplish all data manipulation and analysis in SAS. The Log window is where SAS software communicates with the user about its work; as syntax is processed, SAS prints an ongoing commentary in the log with respect to the progress of the tasks. Traditionally, the Output window is where any printed product of fully executed syntax (also known as output), such as tables and lists, can be found. In recent versions of SAS software, output is more typically found in the Results Viewer (Figure 1.2b). The Results Viewer, which displays output in HTML format, automatically opens when the first output of a SAS session is created.

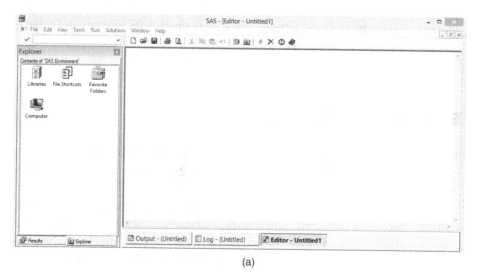

(a)

FIGURE 1.2A. SAS Windowing Environment.

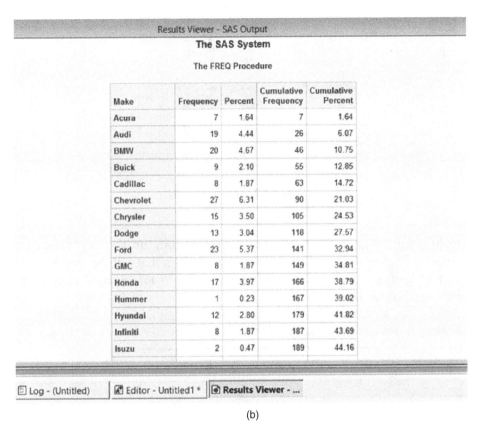

(b)

Figure 1.2b. SAS Results Viewer.

On the bottom left-hand side of the SAS workspace there is another section where the Explorer and Results tabs are located (Figure 1.2a). The Explorer window allows the user to navigate through data libraries and the Results window provides a listing of what is available to view in the results viewer or output window. From the Explorer window, double clicking opens datasets in the Viewtable (Figure 1.3); from the Results window, double-clicking brings the programmer to a specific piece of output.

Editor Window

The editor window is where syntax is written. SAS (running on Microsoft Windows) offers a feature called the 'Enhanced Editor', which is designed

	Make	Model	Type	Origin	Drive Train	MSRP	Invoice	Engine Size (L)	Cylinders
1	Acura	MDX	SUV	Asia	All	$36,945	$33,337	3.5	6
2	Acura	RSX Type S 2dr	Sedan	Asia	Front	$23,820	$21,761	2	4
3	Acura	TSX 4dr	Sedan	Asia	Front	$26,990	$24,647	2.4	4
4	Acura	TL 4dr	Sedan	Asia	Front	$33,195	$30,299	3.2	6
5	Acura	3.5 RL 4dr	Sedan	Asia	Front	$43,755	$39,014	3.5	6
6	Acura	3.5 RL w/Navigation 4dr	Sedan	Asia	Front	$46,100	$41,100	3.5	6
7	Acura	NSX coupe 2dr manual S	Sports	Asia	Rear	$89,765	$79,978	3.2	6
8	Audi	A4 1.8T 4dr	Sedan	Europe	Front	$25,940	$23,508	1.8	4
9	Audi	A41.8T convertible 2dr	Sedan	Europe	Front	$35,940	$32,506	1.8	4
10	Audi	A4 3.0 4dr	Sedan	Europe	Front	$31,840	$28,846	3	6
11	Audi	A4 3.0 Quattro 4dr manual	Sedan	Europe	All	$33,430	$30,366	3	6
12	Audi	A4 3.0 Quattro 4dr auto	Sedan	Europe	All	$34,480	$31,388	3	6
13	Audi	A6 3.0 4dr	Sedan	Europe	Front	$36,640	$33,129	3	6
14	Audi	A6 3.0 Quattro 4dr	Sedan	Europe	All	$39,640	$35,992	3	6
15	Audi	A4 3.0 convertible 2dr	Sedan	Europe	Front	$42,490	$38,325	3	6

FIGURE **1.3. SAS Viewtable.**

to help the programmer debug their programming on the fly. Within the enhanced editor, text is shown in different colors that tell the programmer if their syntax is correct. Below (Example 1.1) is an example of how the enhanced editor works.

EXAMPLE **1.1. Reviewing the Enhanced Editor.**

Syntax	Result
`libname x 'example1';`	✔
`libnm x 'example1';`	✖
`libname x example1';`	✖

The first line shows correct syntax. The word 'libname', when typed into the enhanced editor, will appear in blue because it is a recognized SAS command, and the path 'example 1' will appear in purple because it is fully enclosed by single quotes, telling SAS it is a character string. In the second line we see that 'libnm' is spelled incorrectly; the misspelled syntax will appear in red because it is not a recognized SAS command. In the third line the missing quote before *example 1* renders the path unidentifiable as a character string.

Log Window

Although the enhanced editor is helpful, it is not foolproof. Often, simple spelling errors such as those in Example 1.1 are not initially identified by the programmer. Fortunately, the log is another place where we can and should frequently check our work.

SAS uses the log to tell the programmer how things are going. It is a documentation of everything that happens during the SAS session. Periodically checking the log can save a great deal of time later. The three most common types of messages are NOTE, ERROR, and WARNING. Line numbers are included in some messages to indicate the exact point in the program where an error occurred.

"Note" appears in blue. It describes system processing times and information describing the datasets involved in a particular process. This is a useful place to check the efficiency of your program (by looking at the processing time) and to make sure your dataset has the correct number of observations and variables (Output 1.1).

OUTPUT 1.1. SAS Log: Example of Note Message.

```
NOTE: There were 15 observations read from the data set SASUSER.HOUSES.
NOTE: The data set WORK.X has 15 observations and 6 variables.
NOTE: DATA statement used (Total process time):
      real time           0.20 seconds
      cpu time            0.01 seconds
```

"Error" appears in red. It identifies a problem that caused SAS to stop running. Output 1.2 indicates a filename problem; usually this type of error indicates a problem with the path that is specified on the filename statement.

OUTPUT 1.2. SAS Log: Example of Error Message.

```
ERROR: Error in the FILENAME statement.
```

Output 1.3 shows an example where a dataset 'work.xyz' has been called upon but does not exist at the specified location.

OUTPUT 1.3. SAS Log: Example of Error Message.

```
ERROR: File WORK.XYX.DATA does not exist.
```

"Warning" appears in green. This alerts the user to potential hazards or missteps in data handling. The warning statement should be read carefully; common warnings are due to nonmatching variable lengths, incomplete datasets, and the halt of data steps before completion. Each message gives the user a reference to where the message comes from and describes its meaning and possible options for correcting the issue.

Output 1.4 indicates a warning explaining that the dataset work practice may be incomplete, noting that the dataset has zero observations and zero variables. The warning message makes it clear that the data step needs to be debugged.

OUTPUT 1.4. SAS Log: Example of Warning.

```
WARNING: The data set WORK.PRACTICE may be incomplete.  When this step was stopped there were
         0 observations and 0 variables.
```

Output 1.5 shows a product expiration issue. The SAS system operates in 'warning mode' when the product license is close to its expiration date.

OUTPUT 1.5. SAS Log: Example of Warning.

```
WARNING: The Base SAS Software product with which RESULTS is associated will be expiring soon,
WARNING: and is currently in warning mode to indicate this upcoming expiration. Please run
WARNING: PROC SETINIT to obtain more information on your warning period.
```

Log messages are particularly important because they offer information that may not be obvious. Often a new dataset is created or output is produced but it is inaccurate or incomplete due to a programming error. Log messages can tell the programmer when this is the case.

Explorer Window and Viewtable

The explorer window allows us to navigate through SAS libraries and catalogs as well as the computer's libraries, drives, and devices (explained in greater detail in Chapter 3). Double-clicking on each library reveals included SAS datasets. While the Explorer Window is active, the view menu allows the user to toggle between various versions of list and thumbnail views. The 'Up one level' button is also available when the Explorer Window is active. This button

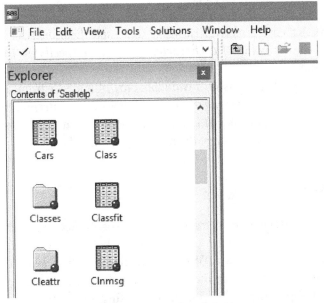

FIGURE 1.4. 'Up One Level' Button.

allows the user to navigate out of one library and into another (Figure 1.4). Double-clicking on a dataset from the Explorer Window opens that dataset in the Viewtable (Figure 1.3). If the explorer window is not already open (or it is accidentally closed), reopen the window by toggling to 'view' on the toolbar and select 'contents only'. Further discussions of investigating data in the Viewtable can be found in Chapter 2.

Accessing Data for This Book

To further demonstrate the Explorer and Viewtable windows, let's take a look at the datasets we will be using for examples throughout this book. First, navigate to the Explorer tab, double-click on the 'Libraries' icon, and then open the folder labeled 'Sashelp.' Scroll through the listing of datasets. Locate the datasets labeled 'Cars', 'Shoes', and 'Class'. We will begin with 'Cars'; double-click on it. The Viewtable should open in the right-hand workspace of the SAS window and the 'Cars' dataset should be visible.

Simple SAS Tips for New Programmers

- *Syntax is not case sensitive. However, case specification is necessary when calling upon the value of a character variable or specifying the path to an external file.*
- *Check the log! The log is an invaluable part of the SAS framework; it saves time and gives the programmer an idea of how SAS is interpreting the code.*
- *Punctuation is important. ALL statements end with a semicolon. A mark as simple as a period can change the meaning of text.*

DATA MIGRATION

Data stored in alternative formats (e.g., Microsoft Access, Microsoft Excel, text files) must be converted to SAS format before any manipulation can be done using SAS software. When data manipulation is complete, many datasets must be exported to these alternative formats. There are a few common ways of importing and exporting data using SAS. The import and export wizards provide simple, point-and-click avenues, while composing and executing syntax using the import and export procedures (PROC IMPORT, PROC EXPORT) provides a more hands-on approach. In this chapter we will describe the Import wizard and the IMPORT procedure. Similar techniques apply to exporting data using the Export wizard and EXPORT procedure. In Chapter 8, we will discuss another option when we present JMP software as an alternative for importing data with unusual formats.

The Wizard

Using the wizard to import data files is an easy and efficient way of bringing external data into SAS. Files can be imported from various formats such as Microsoft Access, Microsoft Excel, and text files. Open the 'File' menu on the top left of the SAS toolbar and select 'import data.' The following screen appears (Figure 1.5); the wizard would like to know "What type of data do you wish to import?"

After choosing the type of file to be imported, the wizard prompts for the location of the file using the 'browse' button. In the next step a SAS destination is selected, the default is the 'work' folder, and 'Member' indicates how SAS should name the dataset.

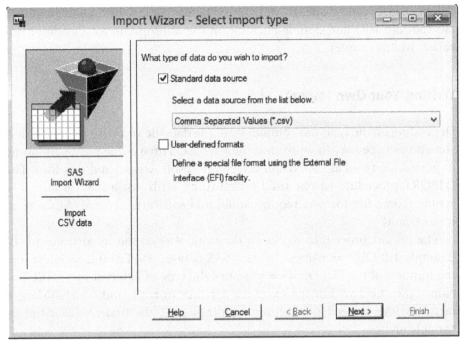

FIGURE 1.5. Import Wizard.

The next screen asks the question of whether or not you would like to save your syntax. If the program you are creating is going to be run again, then yes, it is always a good idea to save the syntax. You can choose any location you like to save the information. One option is to maintain a single SAS program for this purpose and append all imports to this single program. Once the import process is complete and syntax is saved, it can be copied into the current program. If the import will never be used again, then saving the syntax may be a useless task. The decision is completely up to the programmer and their future needs.

The wizard will exit after completion of the import process; if import has been successful, then a new dataset is available. The log is a good place to determine the status of the import (Output 1.6). It will reveal whether the dataset was created and the path to its location.

OUTPUT 1.6. SAS Log: Data Set Creation.

```
NOTE: WORK.SAMPLE_DATA data set was successfully created.
NOTE: The data set WORK.SAMPLE_DATA has 4 observations and 3 variables.
```

The dataset can be opened and viewed by navigating through the explorer tab (bottom left) and double-clicking on the appropriate icon as described earlier in this chapter.

Writing Your Own Import

Depending on the type and complexity of the data file you wish to import, it is sometimes necessary to write your own syntax. Three of the most commonly imported file types are Microsoft Excel, Microsoft Access, and text files. The IMPORT procedure can be used for all three, with just a few variations in syntax (some file formats require additional software, i.e., SAS/ACCESS to import data).

The import procedure works in the same way as the import wizard. In Example 1.2 OUT = names the new SAS dataset, DATAFILE = references the location of the file, DBMS = specifies the type of external file, SHEET = names the sheet within the excel file for SAS to read, and GETNAMES = instructs SAS to read the column headings (i.e., the first row of data) as variable names.

EXAMPLE 1.2. Importing Data from Microsoft Excel Using the IMPORT Procedure.

```
PROC IMPORT OUT= WORK.Sample
DATAFILE= "C:\Desktop\exceldata_ch1P2.xlsx"
DBMS=xlsx REPLACE;
SHEET="sheet1";
GETNAMES=YES;
RUN;
```

Similar to Example 1.2, the syntax shown in Example 1.3 imports a text file. The one difference is the inclusion of "DATAROW," which tells SAS to start reading data from the specified row number.

EXAMPLE 1.3 Importing Data from a Text File Using the IMPORT Procedure.

```
PROC IMPORT OUT= WORK.Sample
DATAFILE= "C:\Desktop\txtsas.txt";
DBMS=TAB REPLACE;
GETNAMES=YES;
DATAROW=2;
RUN;
```

Example 1.4 shows syntax for importing a file from a Microsoft Access database. DATABASE = is similar to DATAFILE = in that it references the location of the database. SCANMEMO = scans for the length of the longest string and uses that for the variable lengths.

EXAMPLE 1.4 Importing Data from a Microsoft Access Table Using the IMPORT Procedure.

```
PROC IMPORT OUT=WORK.access_table
DATATABLE= "tablename"
DBMS=ACCESS REPLACE;
DATABASE=" C:\Desktop\accesstable.accdb";
SCANMEMO=YES;
RUN;
```

Regardless of which technique is employed, it is important to remember to check the log for errors and to check new datasets visually to be sure the resulting dataset meets expectations.

NAVIGATING ENTERPRISE GUIDE

Enterprise Guide (EG) is an alternative platform for SAS programming, which offers the same functionality as traditional SAS windows in a GUI interface. Drop-down menus in EG allow the user to browse procedures, options, and functions with which to execute both simple and advanced statistical analysis. In short, anything that can be accomplished in Base SAS can also be accomplished in EG, using the drop-down menus or by manually entering syntax into the program window.

Although EG and the SAS Windowing Environment are grounded in the same programming and analysis software, the two working environments are different. The default arrangement of the windows in EG is displayed in Figure 1.6. As with most software packages, the visual appearance of the windows and buttons in EG can be specified to the user's liking. In general, there are three spaces: the project tree, the resources pane, and the workspace.

All work in EG is organized and stored by project. The project tree provides a snapshot of all of the programs, tasks, results, and datasets associated with a specific project. In general, work can be divided into as many or as few projects as you choose; however, only one project can be open at a time. Clicking on an item in the project tree brings it up in the workspace. For

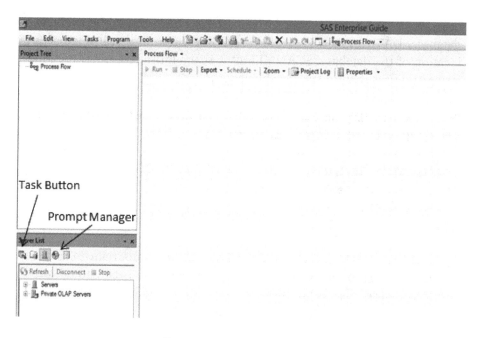

FIGURE 1.6. Enterprise Guide.

instance, if a program is selected, it will appear in the workspace, which will function as an enhanced editor as long as the program is selected. If a dataset is selected, it will appear as a table in the workspace.

One special feature of EG is the process flow. Selecting Process Flow in the project tree brings up a schematic of all items associated with the project, which is displayed in the workspace. The user can also open items from the process flow schematic by double-clicking. In any given project there can be any number of process flows.

The resource pane functions as the command center for EG and houses a handful of useful tools. Two unique tools are the task listing and the prompt manager. Clicking on the task button calls upon a list of tasks that can be selected and executed. Tasks include but are not limited to creating charts/graphs, sorting data, running analyses, and creating libraries. Since EG gives us the ability to save and rerun an entire project repeatedly, it also allows the inclusion of prompts to restrict the parameters of the project based on one or more variables. The prompt manager gives the user quick access to any prompts that they have built into the project.

In this book we will end our discussion of EG by reiterating that it is an alternative to standard programming in SAS, which harnesses the power of SAS analytics in a more menu- and mouse-driven interface. If you determine that EG is the right option for you, we recommend referencing *The Little SAS Book for Enterprise Guide* by Slaughter and Delwiche for a more in-depth explanation of the options in EG.

CHAPTER 2

Preliminary Data Exploration

Once a dataset is available in SAS, the next logical step is for the programmer to maximize his/her familiarity with that new information in order to optimally clean, maintain, manipulate, or report on the data. The purpose of this chapter is to become comfortable exploring data in SAS. We will build on the navigation skills we learned in Chapter 1 and lay the foundation for understanding SAS datasets and all of their components. Smaller sets of data can be explored visually using the SAS Viewtable; however, most datasets are too large for this method and require a more systematic approach. For this purpose, we recommend the CONTENTS procedure, which provides useful information with respect to the dimensions of a datatable and variable characteristics. In later chapters we will discuss other procedures such as MEANS and FREQUENCY, which provide more in-depth information about variable values.

EXPLORER AND VIEWTABLE WINDOWS

The most straightforward approach to examining a new dataset is to open it in the Viewtable and visually examine the data. Once the Viewtable is open, SAS offers a variety of tools that can help the programmer familiarize themselves with the data.

Navigating in the Explorer and Opening a Dataset in the Viewtable

The Explorer window allows the user to navigate folders and locate datasets using standard mouse-click techniques. Within the view menu, the programmer can choose to view available datasets in list or thumbnail form. When the explorer window is active, the up one level button offers the ability to climb out of one library and into another (see Figure 1.4). Double-clicking on a dataset opens that dataset in a separate window called the Viewtable, which opens in the space on the right-hand side of the screen. In this section we will use a dataset from the sashelp library. Let's begin by opening the 'cars' dataset in the Viewtable. From within the Explorer window click sequentially Libraries>Sashelp>Cars.

Investigating a Dataset in the Viewtable

Once a dataset is open in the Viewtable, there are a number of ways to investigate its elements. Using the scrollbars along the bottom and right side of the window brings the user to the unseen edges of the dataset. Each line of data is referred to as an "observation" and each column is referred to as a "variable." Along the leftmost edge of the Viewtable is a line-by-line observation count, and the top row of data provides variable names or user-defined headings referred to as "labels." Scrolling all the way to the bottom reveals the total number of observations, while scrolling all the way to the right provides some information about the kind of data within the dataset.

Right-clicking on a cell in the top row opens a drop-down menu. The first two options (color and font) refer to the visual appearance of the column headings. The sort, hide, and hold buttons allow for simple manipulation of the dataset. Sort can be ascending or descending, hide actually hides a column, and hold keeps one column locked in place when scrolling to view the rightmost columns. Selecting column description lists the variable attributes at the bottom of the SAS window.

	Make	Model	Type	Origin	Drive Train	MSRP	Invoice	Engine Size (L)
1	Acura	MDX	SUV	Asia	All	$36,945	$33,337	3.5
2	Acura	RSX Type S 2dr	Sedan	Asia	Front	$23,820	$21,761	2
3	Acura	TSX 4dr	Sedan	Asia	Front	$26,990	$24,647	2.4
4	Acura	TL 4dr	Sedan	Asia	Front	$33,195	$30,299	3.2
5	Acura	3.5 RL 4dr	Sedan	Asia	Front	$43,755	$39,014	3.5
6	Acura	3.5 RL w/Navigation 4dr	Sedan	Asia	Front	$46,100	$41,100	3.5
7	Acura	NSX coupe 2dr manual S	Sports	Asia	Rear	$89,765	$79,978	3.2
8	Audi	A4 1.8T 4dr	Sedan	Europe	Front	$25,940	$23,508	1.8
9	Audi	A41.8T convertible 2dr	Sedan	Europe	Front	$35,940	$32,506	1.8
10	Audi	A4 3.0 4dr	Sedan	Europe	Front	$31,840	$28,846	3
11	Audi	A4 3.0 Quattro 4dr manual	Sedan	Europe	All	$33,430	$30,366	3
12	Audi	A4 3.0 Quattro 4dr auto	Sedan	Europe	All	$34,480	$31,388	3
13	Audi	A6 3.0 4dr	Sedan	Europe	Front	$36,640	$33,129	3
14	Audi	A6 3.0 Quattro 4dr	Sedan	Europe	All	$39,640	$35,992	3
15	Audi	A4 3.0 convertible 2dr	Sedan	Europe	Front	$42,490	$38,325	3
16	Audi	A4 3.0 Quattro convertible 2dr	Sedan	Europe	All	$44,240	$40,075	3
17	Audi	A6 2.7 Turbo Quattro 4dr	Sedan	Europe	All	$42,840	$38,840	2.7
18	Audi	A6 4.2 Quattro 4dr	Sedan	Europe	All	$49,690	$44,936	4.2
19	Audi	A8 L Quattro 4dr	Sedan	Europe	All	$69,190	$64,740	4.2
20	Audi	S4 Quattro 4dr	Sedan	Europe	All	$48,040	$43,556	4.2
21	Audi	RS 6 4dr	Sports	Europe	Front	$84,600	$76,417	4.2
22	Audi	TT 1.8 convertible 2dr (coupe)	Sports	Europe	Front	$35,940	$32,512	1.8
23	Audi	TT 1.8 Quattro 2dr (convertible)	Sports	Europe	All	$37,390	$33,891	1.8
24	Audi	TT 3.2 coupe 2dr (convertible)	Sports	Europe	All	$40,590	$36,739	3.2
25	Audi	A6 3.0 Avant Quattro	Wagon	Europe	All	$40,840	$37,060	3
26	Audi	S4 Avant Quattro	Wagon	Europe	All	$49,090	$44,446	4.2
27	BMW	X3 3.0i	SUV	Europe	All	$37,000	$33,873	3

FIGURE 2.1. Dataset in the Viewtable.

The Data and View Menus

Another way to visually explore data in the Viewtable is by using the Data drop-down menu at the top of the SAS window. For instance, selecting 'Hide/Unhide' from this drop-down menu opens a dialogue window where the user can select which columns to hide or unhide from a list of all columns in the dataset.

Selecting 'column attributes' from the drop-down menu opens a window containing useful information about the way the variable is stored by SAS. 'Name' refers to the variable name; this is the name by which the user calls upon the variable in syntax. 'Label' refers to a user-supplied custom description of the variable; 'Length' is the number of bytes, which can also be described as how many character spaces the variable can accommodate; Format provides information about the way variable values will be displayed; and Informat describes the way SAS reads a value as it is brought into the

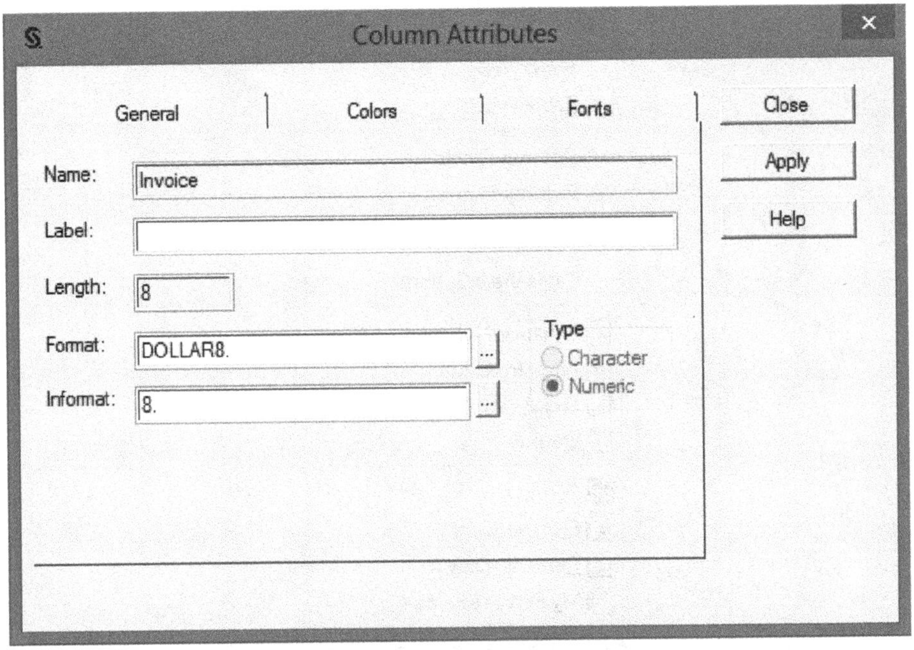

FIGURE 2.2. Column Attributes Window.

dataset. Finally, each variable is stored as either character or numeric; this information can also be found in the Column Attributes Window.

By default, the Viewtable uses 'label' as the column heading. This can be changed by opening the View menu on the toolbar and selecting 'Column_Names' (see Figure 2.3). If a label has not been customized for a particular variable, then the variable name will appear at the top of the column.

Edit Mode and the Where Expression

Clicking in the upper leftmost cell of the Viewtable selects the entire table, and right-clicking on that cell reveals another drop-down menu. Selecting Edit Mode allows the programmer to make changes to the dataset from within the table. Unlike many other software packages, there is no 'undo' button when using edit mode. Edits made to a data table are final and SAS does not maintain any record of changes made. Selecting Where opens another window (see Figure 2.4), which allows the user to specify certain characteristics of

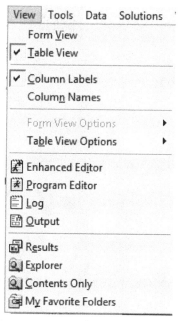

FIGURE 2.3. View Drop-Down Menu.

observations and limit the appearance of data to those that match specifically. Subsetting data in the Where window does not make changes to the dataset or create a new dataset. The Where window is a way to examine only those observations that meet certain criteria.

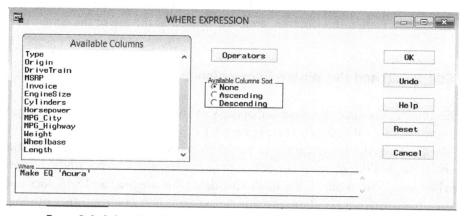

FIGURE 2.4. Subsetting Observations Using the 'Where' Expression Window.

VIEWTABLE: Sashelp.Cars (2004 Car Data)

	Make	Model	Type	Origin	DriveTrain	MSRP	Invoice	Engine Size (L)
1	Acura	MDX	SUV	Asia	All	$36,945	$33,337	3.5
2	Acura	RSX Type S 2dr	Sedan	Asia	Front	$23,820	$21,761	2
3	Acura	TSX 4dr	Sedan	Asia	Front	$26,990	$24,647	2.4
4	Acura	TL 4dr	Sedan	Asia	Front	$33,195	$30,299	3.2
5	Acura	3.5 RL 4dr	Sedan	Asia	Front	$43,755	$39,014	3.5
6	Acura	3.5 RL w/Navigation 4dr	Sedan	Asia	Front	$46,100	$41,100	3.5
7	Acura	NSX coupe 2dr manual S	Sports	Asia	Rear	$89,765	$79,978	3.2

FIGURE 2.5. Subset of Observations Where 'Make' Is 'Acura.'

Consider a request to identify all observations in the 'Cars' dataset where the variable make is defined as Acura. First, click the upper left cell in the Viewtable, then right-click to reveal a drop-down menu. Then, select Edit Mode, right-click again to reveal the same drop-down menu, and this time select Where. The window in Figure 2.4 will appear. Selecting the variable 'make' in the list, EQ from the list of operators, '<LOOKUP distinct values>', 'Acura', and then OKAY will produce a subset of the data including only the observations where 'make' = 'Acura' (see Figure 2.5).

To clear the Where selection, the programmer has two options. The simplest way is to close the Viewtable window; when it is reopened, the complete dataset will once again be visible. The alternative is to right-click in the upper left (blank) cell of the open Viewtable and select 'Where Clear' from the drop-down menu.

THE CONTENTS PROCEDURE

Often a programmer receives a dataset and knows virtually nothing about it. We have learned that one option for becoming familiar with new data is to open it in the Viewtable and visually scroll through the actual data, viewing variable names, labels, and values. With very large datasets, this is an impractical way to become acquainted with the data. An alternative is to begin exploration of a new dataset with the Contents Procedure, otherwise known as PROC CONTENTS. This procedure provides descriptive information about a dataset that can be viewed in the output window or results viewer. PROC CONTENTS offers a snapshot of the number of observations and variables as well as names, types, formats, informats, and labels of all variables in the dataset.

Sample Syntax for the CONTENTS Procedure

Let's further investigate the 'Cars' dataset using PROC CONTENTS. First, copy the syntax below into the editor window.

EXAMPLE 2.1. Syntax for the CONTENTS Procedure.

```
proc contents data = sashelp.cars; run;
```

You may notice that the word 'Run' appears at the end of the syntax followed by a semicolon. To successfully submit SAS syntax, it must always be followed by a RUN statement. Once the syntax is written, click the running person button located on the toolbar or navigate to the menu ribbon and click Run > Submit to instruct SAS to execute the commands.

Reviewing the Output

Automatically, the output window and the results viewer will be populated with identical material relating to the structure of the dataset. The results viewer is a fourth window that only appears when executed syntax produces readable output. Three sections of information are included in the standard output for PROC CONTENTS: dataset (Figure 2.6), engine (Figure 2.7), and variable (Figure 2.8).

Valuable information at the dataset level is circled in Figure 2.6. Data Set Name indicates that the output reflects data from the SASHELP library and that the name of the dataset is CARS. Label is the user-defined label of the dataset; most work datasets tend to not be labeled so this field frequently appears as blank. One benefit of labeling datasets is that it can make it easier to understand their contents with little effort. Observations are the number of observations read. Variables are the number of unique variables included. Sorted indicates if the data is sorted; the value of 'yes' indicates sorting has been done.

Figure 2.7 shows the engine/host dependent information. While this is a standard portion of the output for PROC CONTENTS, the content of this table is not useful to the scope of this book. Therefore, we will move to the variable information shown in Figure 2.8.

Figure 2.8 shows the last portion of the contents procedure output, which lists all variables stored in the dataset along with pertinent attributes

The SAS System

The CONTENTS Procedure

Data Set Name	SASHELP.CARS	Observations	428
Member Type	DATA	Variables	15
Engine	V9	Indexes	0
Created	06/20/2013 00:38:06	Observation Length	152
Last Modified	06/20/2013 00:38:06	Deleted Observations	0
Protection		Compressed	NO
Data Set Type		Sorted	YES
Label	2004 Car Data		
Data Representation	WINDOWS_64		
Encoding	us-ascii ASCII (ANSI)		

FIGURE 2.6. Contents Procedure Output: Dataset Information.

including position, name, type, length, format, and label. Position (#) is an indicator of the order in which variables are stored. Type specifies whether the variable is character or numeric. As we learn to manipulate data in SAS, the variable information provided by PROC CONTENTS will prove

Engine/Host Dependent Information	
Data Set Page Size	65536
Number of Data Set Pages	2
First Data Page	1
Max Obs per Page	430
Obs in First Data Page	413
Number of Data Set Repairs	0
ExtendObsCounter	YES
Filename	C:\Program Files\SASHome2\SASFoundation\9.4\core\sashelp\cars.sas7bdat
Release Created	9.0401B0
Host Created	X64_7PRO

FIGURE 2.7. Contents Procedure Output: Engine/Host Information.

| Alphabetic List of Variables and Attributes | | | | |
# Variable	Type	Len	Format	Label
9 Cylinders	Num	8		
5 DriveTrain	Char	5		
8 EngineSize	Num	8		Engine Size (L)
10 Horsepower	Num	8		
7 Invoice	Num	8	DOLLAR8.	
15 Length	Num	8		Length (IN)
11 MPG_City	Num	8		MPG (City)
12 MPG_Highway	Num	8		MPG (Highway)
6 MSRP	Num	8	DOLLAR8.	
1 Make	Char	13		
2 Model	Char	40		
4 Origin	Char	6		
3 Type	Char	8		
13 Weight	Num	8		Weight (LBS)
14 Wheelbase	Num	8		Wheelbase (IN)

FIGURE 2.8. Contents Procedure Output: Variable Information.

invaluable. This portion of the output can be compared with the variable attributes data discussed in Figure 2.2.

Options for the CONTENTS Procedure

When employing most SAS procedures, it is beneficial to have a working understanding of the options that SAS offers. Options are a way to customize SAS output for any procedure in order to more effectively meet the needs of the project at hand. In a procedure statement, options directly follow the name of the procedure and are listed before the closing semicolon. In fact, in Example 2.1 the 'data = ' syntax is actually an option that is used to specify the input dataset for the contents procedure. In most cases, there are multiple options available; in this book we will limit our conversation to those that are most common and useful.

As specified in the prior section, default order of variables in PROC CONTENTS output is alphabetical and case sensitive (all variables beginning with an uppercase letter are listed, followed by all variables beginning with a lowercase letter). Depending on the task at hand, it is sometimes useful to list the variables in an alternative order. In Example 2.2 we use VARNUM as our sort order for the variable listing. In this example, SAS will list the variables in order of position (Figure 2.9).

EXAMPLE **2.2. Contents Procedure Syntax with VARNUM option.**

```
proc contents data = sashelp.cars varnum; run;
```

Variables in Creation Order				
#	Variable	Type	Len	Format	Label
1	Make	Char	13		
2	Model	Char	40		
3	Type	Char	8		
4	Origin	Char	6		
5	DriveTrain	Char	5		
6	MSRP	Num	8	DOLLAR8.	
7	Invoice	Num	8	DOLLAR8.	
8	EngineSize	Num	8		Engine Size (L)
9	Cylinders	Num	8		
10	Horsepower	Num	8		
11	MPG_City	Num	8		MPG (City)
12	MPG_Highway	Num	8		MPG (Highway)
13	Weight	Num	8		Weight (LBS)
14	Wheelbase	Num	8		Wheelbase (IN)
15	Length	Num	8		Length (IN)

FIGURE **2.9. CONTENTS Procedure Output with VARNUM Option.**

SAS also offers the ORDER = option as a way for the user to control the order in which variables are printed. Specifying ORDER = IGNORECASE (Example 2.3) creates a variable listing in alphabetical order ignoring the case. This option can be helpful when a dataset contains a large number of variables with similar variable names.

EXAMPLE 2.3. CONTENTS Procedure Syntax with IGNORECASE Option.

```
proc contents data = foldername.datasetname order =
ignorecase; run;
```

Another way that we use options is to request more information than the SAS default provides. For instance, in the Contents Procedure we can use the options DIRECTORY and DETAILS to ask SAS for more information than is standard. In Example 2.4 we use DIRECTORY to request a listing of all datasets found in the library, and in Example 2.5 we combine the DIRECTORY option with the DETAILS option to provide some simple information about those datasets. The resulting outputs include not only the standard contents output but an additional page, with information about the library in which the specified dataset resides. These additional pages (first ten observations only) are displayed in Figures 2.10 and 2.11 for Examples 2.4 and 2.5, respectively.

EXAMPLE 2.4. CONTENTS Procedure Syntax with DIRECTORY Option.

```
proc contents data = sashelp.cars directory; run;
```

EXAMPLE 2.5. CONTENTS Procedure Syntax for DIRECTORY Option with DETAILS.

```
proc contents data = sasuser.build directory details; run;
```

Despite the multitude of approaches available to the programmer, there is no right or wrong way to begin exploring data in SAS. The methods for dataset investigation described in this chapter provide options for beginning an iterative process of familiarizing oneself with a new dataset in SAS. SAS provides a number of additional procedures that are also useful tools in data exploration, which will be covered in later chapters. The goal of the methods described in this chapter is to help the programmer determine which aspects of new data require further exploration. For instance, when faced with a new dataset comprised of 2 variables and 20 observations, a visual exploration in the Viewtable is most likely sufficient and no further methods are required.

#	Name	Member Type	Level	File Size	Last Modified
1	AACOMP	DATA	3	393216	06/20/2013 00:51:32
	AACOMP	INDEX		128000	06/20/2013 00:51:32
2	AARFM	DATA	2	262144	06/20/2013 00:52:35
	AARFM	INDEX		17408	06/20/2013 00:52:35
3	AC	CATALOG	2	17408	06/20/2013 00:54:57
4	ADSMSG	DATA	2	262144	06/20/2013 00:54:18
	ADSMSG	INDEX		37888	06/20/2013 00:54:18
5	AFCLASS	CATALOG	2	1979392	06/20/2013 00:55:55
6	AFMSG	DATA	2	458752	06/20/2013 00:51:36
	AFMSG	INDEX		74752	06/20/2013 00:51:36
7	AFTOOLS	CATALOG	2	2323456	06/20/2013 00:55:55
8	ASSCMGR	DATA	2	327680	06/20/2013 01:01:27
9	BASE	CATALOG	2	697344	06/20/2013 00:52:35
10	BMT	DATA	2	131072	06/20/2013 01:03:40

FIGURE 2.10. CONTENTS Procedure Output with DIRECTORY Option.

In contrast, an entirely new library chock full of new datasets more likely necessitates a PROC CONTENTS employing the directory and details options, followed by a series of PROC CONTENTS performed on each individual dataset listed.

#	Name	Member Type	Level	Obs, Entries or Indexes	Vars	Label	File Size	Last Modified
1	AACOMP	DATA	3	1530	4		393216	06/20/2013 00:51:32
	AACOMP	INDEX		1			128000	06/20/2013 00:51:32
2	AARFM	DATA	2	56	4		262144	06/20/2013 00:52:35
	AARFM	INDEX		1			17408	06/20/2013 00:52:35
3	AC	CATALOG	2	0			17408	06/20/2013 00:54:57
4	ADSMSG	DATA	2	426	6		262144	06/20/2013 00:54:18
	ADSMSG	INDEX		2			37888	06/20/2013 00:54:18
5	AFCLASS	CATALOG	2	0			1979392	06/20/2013 00:55:55
6	AFMSG	DATA	2	1090	6		458752	06/20/2013 00:51:36
	AFMSG	INDEX		2			74752	06/20/2013 00:51:36
7	AFTOOLS	CATALOG	2	0			2323456	06/20/2013 00:55:55
8	ASSCMGR	DATA	2	402	19		327680	06/20/2013 01:01:27
9	BASE	CATALOG	2	0			697344	06/20/2013 00:52:35
10	BMT	DATA	2	137	3	Bone Marrow Transplant Patients	131072	06/20/2013 01:03:40

FIGURE 2.11. CONTENTS Procedure Output with DIRECTORY and DETAILS Options.

TEST YOUR SKILLS

Use the sashelp dataset 'class' and the techniques described in Chapter 2 to accomplish the following tasks:

2.1 Visually explore the dataset in the Viewtable.
2.2 Determine if the variable 'weight' is character or numeric.
2.3 Subset the data to include only the female students.
2.4 Use the CONTENTS procedure to determine how the dataset is Labeled.

SOLUTIONS

2.1 Visually explore the dataset in the Viewtable.

VIEWTABLE: Sashelp.Class (Student Data)

	Name	Sex	Age	Height	Weight
1	Alfred	M	14	69	112.5
2	Alice	F	13	56.5	84
3	Barbara	F	13	65.3	98
4	Carol	F	14	62.8	102.5
5	Henry	M	14	63.5	102.5
6	James	M	12	57.3	83
7	Jane	F	12	59.8	84.5
8	Janet	F	15	62.5	112.5
9	Jeffrey	M	13	62.5	84
10	John	M	12	59	99.5
11	Joyce	F	11	51.3	50.5
12	Judy	F	14	64.3	90
13	Louise	F	12	56.3	77
14	Mary	F	15	66.5	112
15	Philip	M	16	72	150
16	Robert	M	12	64.8	128
17	Ronald	M	15	67	133
18	Thomas	M	11	57.5	85
19	William	M	15	66.5	112

2.2 Determine if the variable 'weight' is character or numeric.

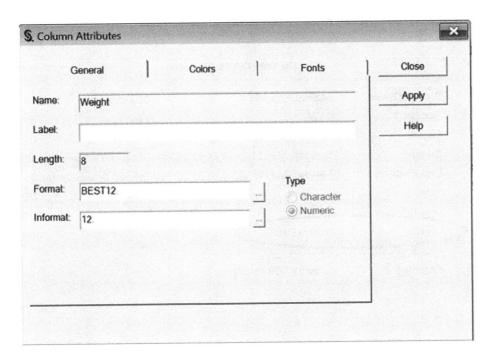

2.3 Subset the data to include only the female students.

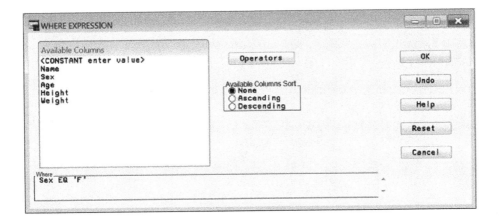

2.4 Use the CONTENTS procedure to determine how the dataset is Labeled.

```
proc contents data = sashelp.class; run;
```

The CONTENTS Procedure

Data Set Name	SASHELP.CLASS	Observations	19
Member Type	DATA	Variables	5
Engine	V9	Indexes	0
Created	Tuesday, May 24, 2011 01:52:28 PM	Observation Length	40
Last Modified	Tuesday, May 24, 2011 01:52:28 PM	Deleted Observations	0
Protection		Compressed	NO
Data Set Type		Sorted	NO
Label	Student Data		
Data Representation	WINDOWS_32		
Encoding	us-ascii ASCII (ANSI)		

CHAPTER 3

Storing and Manipulating Data

In this chapter we will learn about storing and manipulating data in SAS, by considering the structure of datasets and the characteristics of variables. We begin with a description of how to access existing data using the SAS specific library convention, including an overview of the different types of storage SAS offers. The Data step is introduced as the primary method for data manipulation in SAS, punctuated with plenty of sample syntax and illustrative figures providing the user with a thorough understanding of what the Data step can do for a programmer. We then move to variable creation and manipulation including an overview of functions and different ways to transform numeric and character variables.

LIBRARIES, LIBRARY REFERENCES, AND THE LIBNAME STATEMENT

SAS stores and creates data using a library convention. Libraries are a way to call upon a location within the computer by labeling it with a single letter or phrase for the duration of the SAS session. This allows the user a

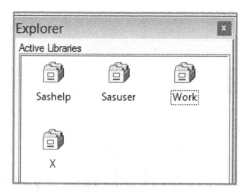

FIGURE **3.1. Active Libraries in the Explorer Window.**

time-saving alternative to repeating a lengthy path name in multiple places. When pulling data from a shared server, the path can include several folders to navigate through before locating the file, for example 'Z:\JK\SAS 2014\Paper2019\Datasets\final'.

In Example 3.1, a LIBNAME statement allows the programmer to write the path once, assigning it the library reference (libref) 'x.' This libref can be used to locate any SAS dataset in that particular folder for the entirety of the SAS session. Library References can consist of one to eight characters and must begin with a letter, a through z, or an underscore (_); remaining characters may consist of letters, numbers, or underscores.

EXAMPLE **3.1. LIBNAME Statement Syntax.**

```
libname x 'Z:\JK\SAS 2014\Paper2019\Datasets\final';
```

One way to view a dataset within an active library is to toggle to the explorer tab and click on the 'Libraries' folder (Figure 3.1). SAS will always show three active libraries, 'Sashelp', 'Sasuser', and 'Work.' The library 'X' was created in Example 3.1 using a libname statement. While the libref 'X' is a temporary shortcut for accessing a specific location, any dataset written to that location using the libref is stored there permanently.

By double-clicking on the desired folder we are able to view its contents. When we open a library in the Explorer window, SAS automatically displays all SAS version 8 or higher datasets stored in that location. Other items in the folder (e.g., Word documents, spreadsheets, etc.) will not be displayed in the Explorer window.

To access data stored in earlier formats, we must create an additional libref (using a separate libname statement) and specify the version (Example 3.2). Using this technique it is possible to assign one physical location as two different libraries. When they are opened in the Explorer, each library will only display datasets of the specified SAS version.

EXAMPLE 3.2. LIBNAME Statement Syntax for Data Stored in Earlier SAS Versions.

```
Libname v6 y 'Z:\JK\SAS 2014\Paper2019\Datasets\final';
```

In a program that will be rerun on another occasion, it is most useful to include LIBNAME statements at the top of the editor window. When the program is reopened, the LIBNAME statement will be run first so that subsequent syntax can be processed with no difficulty locating files. When calling upon the path defined by the LIBNAME statement, indicate the libref, followed by a period and the SAS dataset name (Example 3.3).

EXAMPLE 3.3. Using a Library Reference in Syntax.

```
proc contents data = x.sample; run;
```

TYPES OF DATASETS: TEMPORARY AND PERMANENT

SAS creates and stores two types of datasets: permanent and temporary. Permanent datasets are written to an existing location and are stored in that location beyond the duration of the single SAS session. The SAS library convention, as outlined in the preceding paragraphs, is particularly useful in creating and accessing permanent datasets. Temporary datasets are stored in the 'Work' library and exist only as long as the SAS session during which they are created remains active. In other words, they cannot be used again in a future session unless they are recreated. Both types of datasets can be accessed using the navigation technique outlined previously (Figure 3.1).

THE DATA STEP

Data steps are written by the programmer with the ultimate goal of creating a new SAS dataset. At first thought, creating a new set of data may seem counterintuitive to the task at hand; however, there are many reasons to create a new dataset. The primary reason to create a SAS dataset is to manipulate it. SAS procedures can only be used on SAS datasets; other data formats such as Microsoft Excel or Access, ASCII, and so forth must be migrated to SAS format before any other SAS functionality can be employed. By creating new datasets we can easily add/delete, rename or reformat variables, subset data, combine two or more datasets, or change the location of a preexisting dataset. In this section we will review the anatomy of a SAS Data Step and explore some of its most common functionalities. Further, we will consider frequently employed syntax for those tasks.

Anatomy of Data Step Syntax

The Syntax   **The Explanation**

```
DATA LIBNAME.DATASET;
```

The *Data* statement specifies where and how to store the new dataset as well as what to name it.

```
INPUT ID VAR2 VAR3
FORMATVAR2.;
DATALINES;
01 1 0
;
```

The next portion of the Data Step tells SAS where to find the data. Using a *Datalines* statement allows the programmer to enter data directly into the editor.

```
INFILE 'PATH';
INPUT ID VAR2 VAR3;

SET X Y;

MERGE X Y;
```

In contrast, *Infile*, *Set* or *Merge* statements instruct SAS to pull the data from another location.

```
IF ID > 00;
WHERE ID > 00;
```

Using *Where* and *If* statements we can specify which observations will be included in the new dataset.

```
VAR4 = MAX (VAR2, VAR3);
FORMAT VAR4 YESNO.;
```

Variable manipulation is often the main goal of creating a new dataset and includes creating new variables and formatting, renaming, or re-labeling existing ones.

```
DROP VAR2 VAR3;
KEEP ID VAR4;
```

Final changes to the dimensions of a dataset are often made using *Drop* and *Keep* variables which specify which variables should be included in the new dataset.

```
RUN;
```

A Data Step always ends with the Run command.

DATA Statement

The first line of the DATA step is always the DATA statement. The primary purpose of the DATA statement is to name the dataset and specify how it will be stored. As described previously, the dataset can be stored as either permanent or temporary. If the programmer simply names the dataset, without specifying a location using a LIBREF, the SAS default is to save it in the work folder as a temporary dataset (Example 3.4.1). Alternatively, data can be stored permanently, either by specifying a LIBREF (Example 3.4.2) or writing a full path in single quotes (Example 3.4.3).

EXAMPLE 3.4. **DATA Statement Syntax.**

```
3.4.1    Temporary    data practice1;
3.4.2    Permanent    data x.practice1;
3.4.3    Permanent    data 'c:\folder\subfolder\practice1
                      .sas7bdat';
```

INPUT Statement

The next portion of the data step specifies where the data will come from. There are multiple possibilities for this portion of the data step; the simplest is an INPUT statement, which precedes column format data entry. This is a good time to create mock data for use in this chapter. The data step will create a new dataset that contains only the data specified. The INPUT statement indicates the variable names and informats. The datalines statement followed by a semicolon directs SAS to begin reading subsequent lines as real data.

Enter the following syntax into the enhanced editor to create the datasets 'people1_10' and 'people11_20'. Notice the inclusion of two additional data steps at the end; these are required to format the Date of Birth (DOB) variable. SAS will read this variable as a date (mmddyy10.) because we have instructed it to do so in the input statement. To view it in the dataset as the literal date (mm/dd/yyyy), we must use a format statement in a new data step or procedure. See the section on "Advanced Challenges in Data Manipulation" in Chapter 4 for more information on calendar dates in SAS.

```
data people1_10;
input ID DOB mmddyy10.;
datalines;
1 08/26/1982
2 02/09/1982
3 10/12/2012
4 06/12/1954
5 01/18/1948
6 12/22/1945
7 10/24/1969
8 06/16/1972
9 04/01/1979
10 04/21/1948
;
run;


data people11_20;
input ID DOB mmddyy10.;
datalines;
 11 10/15/1951
 12 12/27/1982
 13 01/25/2010
 14 02/14/1980
 15 03/16/1981
 16 04/17/1982
 17 05/18/1983
 18 06/19/1984
 19 08/18/1957
 20 07/26/1974
 ;
run;


data people1_10;
set people1_10;
format dob mmddyy10.;
run;
```

```
data people11_20;
set people11_20;
format dob mmddyy10.;
run;
```

The syntax above creates the first two SAS datasets. Entering the next portion of syntax (below) creates a third dataset 'Info1_20'. Notice in the input statement, after the variable name "Address" there is specific code that allows for varying lengths of these entries.

```
data Info1_20;
input ID Phone Address $16-37;;
datalines;
 1    2035551892 22 Smith Street
 2    2035553476 173 Main Street
 3    2035556439 59 Green Hill Road
 4    2035557845 87 Jones Hill Road
 5    2035552234 43 West End
 6    2035558453 97B Greystone Lane
 7    2035557654 46 Braintree Boulevard
 8    2035558756 22 Spring Street
 9    2035558897 64 Lovers Lane
10    2035556754 93 James Place
11    2035559985 78 Sistine Way
12    2035554359 101 Apple Street
13    2035558345 91 Colonial Road
14    2035558845 9 Botte Drive
15    2035558642 85 Beechwood Drive
16    2035551357 1579 Durham Road
17    2035550987 84 Anchor Lane
18    2035552689 128 Borrman Road
19    2035557784 104 Montowese Street
20    2035551289 55 Wooding Road
run;
```

INFILE Statement

When the desired dataset already exists in a format other than SAS, we can use the DATA step in combination with an INFILE statement to import the data (Example 3.5). The INFILE statement is typically used with an INPUT statement; the INFILE statement must precede the INPUT statement. The INFILE statement provides SAS with the information to locate the file to be used, and the INPUT statement provides SAS with variable names and other appropriate information for the reading of that file. An alternative to the INFILE statement is the IMPORT procedure, which is discussed in Chapter 1.

EXAMPLE 3.5. DATA Step Syntax with an INFILE Statement.

```
data UsingInfile;
infile 'D:\Work\Info1_20.txt';
input ID Phone Address;
run;
```

SET and MERGE

The SET or MERGE statement tells SAS how to construct the dataset. Using a SET statement instructs SAS to store the specified preexisting SAS dataset in the location determined by the DATA statement. If two or more datasets are listed in a SET statement, they are vertically concatenated in the order they are listed. A MERGE statement replaces the SET statement when horizontally combining observations from two or more SAS datasets into a single new dataset, matched using a unique identifier. In this process, also known as match-merging, the unique identifier is specified with a BY statement, which immediately follows the MERGE statement in the data step.

To explain the difference between a SET and a MERGE, we will use data previously created. Figure 3.2 contains a snapshot of the mock data used in this explanation. The dataset 'People1_10' contains unique identifiers and dates of birth for ten people. 'People11_20' contains unique identifiers and dates of birth for another ten people. The third dataset 'Info1_20' contains addresses and phone numbers for all twenty people.

The best way to create a dataset with all twenty people is to vertically concatenate 'people1_10' with 'people 11_20' using a SET statement (Example 3.6). The resulting dataset is shown in Figure 3.3.

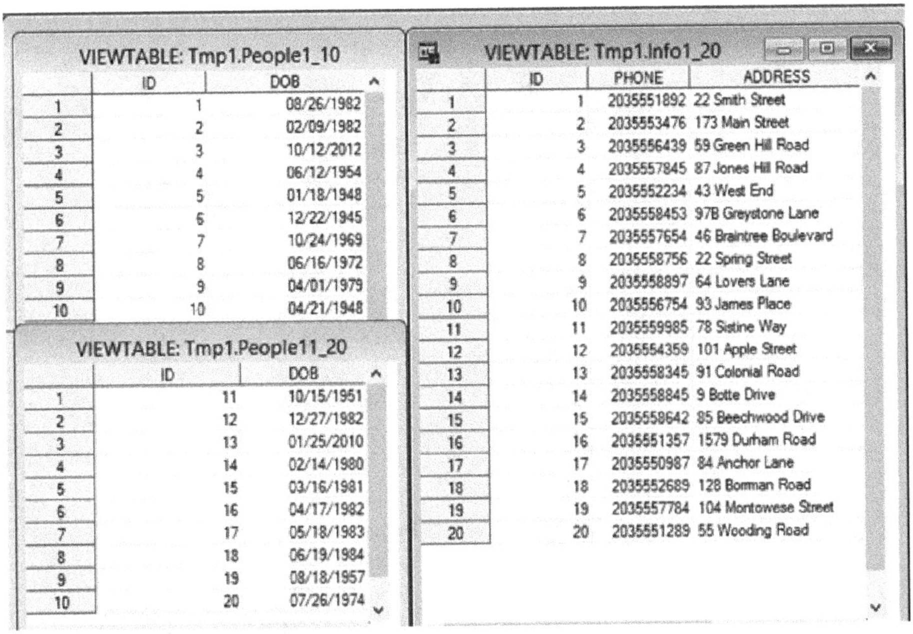

FIGURE 3.2. Sample Datasets: People1_10, People11_20, and Info1_20.

EXAMPLE 3.6. **SET Statement Syntax.**

```
data allpeople;
set people1_10 people11_20;
run;
```

To create a dataset with all twenty people, along with their contact information, a MERGE is performed (Example 3.7), using the dataset we created in Example 3.6. Since a MERGE requires a BY statement, the data must first be sorted according to the variable listed in the BY statement. This is done by including a PROC SORT. The SORT procedure will be discussed in greater detail in Chapter 5.

EXAMPLE 3.7. **MERGE Statement Syntax.**

```
proc sort data = allpeople;
by id;
run;
proc sort data = info1_20;
by id;
run;
```

VIEWTABLE: X.Allpeople

	ID	DOB
1	1	08/26/1982
2	2	02/09/1982
3	3	10/12/2012
4	4	06/12/1954
5	5	01/18/1948
6	6	12/22/1945
7	7	10/24/1969
8	8	06/16/1972
9	9	04/01/1979
10	10	04/21/1948
11	11	10/15/1951
12	12	12/27/1982
13	13	01/25/2010
14	14	02/14/1980
15	15	03/16/1981
16	16	04/17/1982
17	17	05/18/1983
18	18	06/19/1984
19	19	08/18/1957
20	20	07/26/1974

FIGURE 3.3. Dataset Created by Syntax in Example 3.6 Containing All 20 people.

```
data allinfo;
merge allpeople info1_20;
by id;
run;
```

Now, assume that the goal is a dataset with all contact info for only those people in the dataset 'People11_20.' This can be done by performing a MERGE with an IN statement (Example 3.8).

EXAMPLE 3.8. MERGE Statement Syntax with an IN Statement.

```
data info11_20;
merge info1_20 people11_20 (in = a);
by id;
if a;
run;
```

VIEWTABLE: Work.Info11_20				
	ID	PHONE	ADDRESS	DOB
1	11	2035559985	78 Sistine Way	10/15/1951
2	12	2035554359	101 Apple Street	12/27/1982
3	13	2035558345	91 Colonial Road	01/25/2010
4	14	2035558845	9 Botte Drive	02/14/1980
5	15	2035558642	85 Beechwood Drive	03/16/1981
6	16	2035551357	1579 Durham Road	04/17/1982
7	17	2035550987	84 Anchor Lane	05/18/1983
8	18	2035552689	128 Borrman Road	06/19/1984
9	19	2035557784	104 Montowese Street	08/18/1957
10	20	2035551289	55 Wooding Road	07/26/1974

FIGURE 3.4. Dataset Info11_20.

Here, observations are included in the dataset 'info11_20' if the ID value was in the input dataset 'people11_20' (Figure 3.4). Observations with IDs included in 'info1_20' and not included in 'people11_20' are excluded from the new dataset 'info11_20.'

If we excluded the 'in = a' syntax and ran the code as a simple match merge, the resulting dataset would have all twenty people, with missing values for variables found only in the 'people11_20' dataset for IDs not included in that dataset (i.e., observations with ID values 1–10) (Figure 3.5).

Subsetting Variables: DROP and KEEP Statements

Creating a new dataset provides the means to change the dimensions of the dataset by subsetting variables or observations based on specific characteristics. Using a DROP or KEEP statement instructs SAS as to which variables should be excluded or included, respectively, from the new dataset. The dataset sashelp.shoes has seven variables: region, product, subsidiary, stores, sales, inventory, and returns. Now let's assume the goal is to subset that dataset to include only four variables: product, sales, inventory, and returns. This can be accomplished two ways, as shown in Example 3.9.

VIEWTABLE: Work.Info11_20

	ID	PHONE	ADDRESS	DOB
1	1	2035551892	22 Smith Street	
2	2	2035553476	173 Main Street	
3	3	2035556439	59 Green Hill Road	
4	4	2035557845	87 Jones Hill Road	
5	5	2035552234	43 West End	
6	6	2035558453	97B Greystone Lane	
7	7	2035557654	46 Braintree Boulevard	
8	8	2035558756	22 Spring Street	
9	9	2035558897	64 Lovers Lane	
10	10	2035556754	93 James Place	
11	11	2035559985	78 Sistine Way	10/15/1951
12	12	2035554359	101 Apple Street	12/27/1982
13	13	2035558345	91 Colonial Road	01/25/2010
14	14	2035558845	9 Botte Drive	02/14/1980
15	15	2035558642	85 Beechwood Drive	03/16/1981
16	16	2035551357	1579 Durham Road	04/17/1982
17	17	2035550987	84 Anchor Lane	05/18/1983
18	18	2035552689	128 Borrman Road	06/19/1984
19	19	2035557784	104 Montowese Street	08/18/1957
20	20	2035551289	55 Wooding Road	07/26/1974

FIGURE 3.5. **Dataset with All 20 Observations and Missing Values.**

EXAMPLE 3.9. **DROP and KEEP Statement Syntax.**

```
data sub_shoes;
set sashelp.shoes;
drop region subsidiary stores;
run;

data sub_shoes;
set sashelp.shoes;
keep product sales inventory returns;
run;
```

Subsetting Observations: WHERE and IF Statements

Often in data exploration and analysis we want to include only those observations that meet specific criteria. Creating a new dataset is often the easiest way to do this. Example 3.10 uses a WHERE statement to limit the data to only those observations where store is equal to 12.

EXAMPLE 3.10. WHERE Statement Syntax.

```
data temp;
set sashelp.shoes;
where stores = 12;
run;
```

According to the log message shown in Output 3.1, SAS read six observations from the dataset sashelp.shoes where the store was equal to 12. The new temporary dataset can be used for quick sub-analyses on this limited number of observations. In this case, reducing the number of observations (from 395 to 14) even allows the user to visually assess the data.

OUTPUT 3.1. SAS Log Message for Dataset Created Using a WHERE Statement.

```
NOTE: There were 14 observations read from the data set SASHELP.SHOES.
      WHERE stores=12;
NOTE: The data set WORK.TEMP has 14 observations and 7 variables.
NOTE: DATA statement used (Total process time):
      real time           0.22 seconds
      cpu time            0.00 seconds
```

It is important to recognize that the WHERE statement is processed by SAS *as the data is brought in* to the new dataset and can therefore only be used in cases where the criteria is determined by a variable that already exists in the dataset specified by the SET or MERGE statements. In cases where the programmer wishes to subset observations based on criteria determined by a variable being brought into the new dataset using an INFILE statement or a variable created during the data step, an IF statement is required.

EXAMPLE 3.11. IF Statement Syntax.

```
data temp;
set sashelp.shoes;
total = sales + inventory;
if total > 100000;
run;
```

OUTPUT 3.2. **OUTPUT 3.2. SAS Log Message for Dataset Created Using an IF Statement.**

```
NOTE: There were 395 observations read from the data set SASHELP.SHOES.
NOTE: The data set WORK.TEMP has 252 observations and 8 variables.
NOTE: DATA statement used (Total process time):
      real time            0.00 seconds
      cpu time             0.00 seconds
```

Creating New Variables

Another reason to create a new dataset is to create new variables. Going back to our sample datasets 'people1_10' and 'people11_20' (Figure 3.2), let's assume that we want to add a variable to each of those datasets to indicate which dataset it came from before we combined them into 'people1_20'. The syntax in Example 3.12 illustrates the simplest way to create a new variable. In this case, an additional variable is created and has the same value for all observations in each new dataset respectively (Figure 3.6).

EXAMPLE 3.12.   Syntax for Creating a New Variable.
```
data people1_10a;
set people1_10;
dataset = 110;
run;


data people11_20a;
set people11_20;
dataset = 1120;
run;
```

VIEWTABLE: Work.People1_10a			
	ID	DOB	dataset
1	1	08/26/1982	110
2	2	02/09/1982	110
3	3	10/12/2012	110
4	4	06/12/1954	110
5	5	01/18/1948	110
6	6	12/22/1945	110
7	7	10/24/1969	110
8	8	06/16/1972	110
9	9	04/01/1979	110
10	10	04/21/1948	110

VIEWTABLE: Work.People11_20a			
	ID	DOB	dataset
1	11	10/15/1951	1120
2	12	12/27/1982	1120
3	13	01/25/2010	1120
4	14	02/14/1980	1120
5	15	03/16/1981	1120
6	16	04/17/1982	1120
7	17	05/18/1983	1120
8	18	06/19/1984	1120
9	19	08/18/1957	1120
10	20	07/26/1974	1120

FIGURE 3.6. New Variable Dataset.

If these two new datasets are vertically concatenated using a SET statement (Example 3.13), the result is a new dataset with 20 observations and 3 variables, where the new variable 'dataset' indicates the source dataset for each observation.

EXAMPLE 3.13. Syntax for Combining people1_10a and people11_20a.

```
data allpeople_a;
set people1_10a people11_20a;
run;
```

VARIABLE MANIPULATION

Manipulating and/or creating new variables is often necessary when exploring and analyzing a dataset. Frequently variable manipulation is the primary goal of a data step. Variables come in two types: numeric and character. It is pertinent to be knowledgeable of the variable type before beginning to manipulate it. In Chapter 2, we learned how to determine a variable's type from the CONTENTS procedure output. We also learned that if a dataset is open in the Viewtable, it is possible to investigate variable attributes by single-clicking the variable name (or label) from the top row and using the options explained in Figure 2.2.

Numeric Variables

Variables are assumed to be numeric unless otherwise specified during their creation, and take on number values. Numeric variables can be influenced by using simple arithmetic and comparison operators. The symbols $<$, $>$, $=$ $<$, $>$ $=$ and text LT, GT, LE, GE are interchangeable, respectively. Their function definitions are less than, greater than, less than or equal to, and greater than or equal to (Table 3.1). When creating a new numeric variable, we recommend first setting all values to the numeric missing (.). Consider again the dataset 'Shoes' from the Sashelp library. Using this dataset we will take the continuous variable 'Returns' and use it to create a categorical variable named 'Return_Volume'.

Example 3.14 shows two data steps; both will create exactly the same values for the variable 'Return_Volume'. The syntax in Example 3.14 also contains an IF/THEN statement. This type of expression executes syntax for observations that meet the criteria specified. If returns are less than $1,500, then the variable 'Return_Volume' will be set to '0'; if returns are greater than or equal to $1,500, then 'Return_Volume' will be set to '1'. The resulting datasets are identical and can be seen in Figure 3.7.

EXAMPLE 3.14. Creating a New Numeric Variable Using a Comparison Operator.

```
Data Create_Num1;
set sashelp.shoes;
Return_Volume =.;
if returns LT 1500 then Return_Volume = 0;
if returns GE 1500 then Return_Volume = 1;
run;


Data Create_Num2;
set sashelp.shoes;
Return_Volume =.;
if returns < 1500 then Return_Volume = 0;
if returns > = 1500 then Return_Volume = 1;
run;
```

	Region	Product	Subsidiary	Number of Stores	Total Sales	Total Inventory	Total Returns	return_volume
1	Africa	Boot	Addis Ababa	12	$29,761	$191,821	$769	0
2	Africa	Men's Casual	Addis Ababa	4	$67,242	$118,036	$2,284	1
3	Africa	Men's Dress	Addis Ababa	7	$76,793	$136,273	$2,433	1
4	Africa	Sandal	Addis Ababa	10	$62,819	$204,284	$1,861	1
5	Africa	Slipper	Addis Ababa	14	$68,641	$279,795	$1,771	1
6	Africa	Sport Shoe	Addis Ababa	4	$1,690	$16,634	$79	0
7	Africa	Women's Casual	Addis Ababa	2	$51,541	$98,641	$940	0
8	Africa	Women's Dress	Addis Ababa	12	$108,942	$311,017	$3,233	1
9	Africa	Boot	Algiers	21	$21,297	$73,737	$710	0
10	Africa	Men's Casual	Algiers	4	$63,206	$100,982	$2,221	1

FIGURE 3.7. Resulting Datasets Create_Num1 and Create_Num2.

A full list of arithmetic and comparison operators can be found on the support.sas.com website. Table 3.1 presents a list of frequently used comparison operators.

Another common task with numeric variables is to perform arithmetic operations such as addition, subtraction, multiplication, division, and exponentiation as outlined in Table 3.2. When using arithmetic operators, it is important to be aware that the resulting values will be missing (.) if any of the contributing arguments are missing. Often times a SAS function can be used

TABLE 3.1. SAS Comparison Operator Table.

Comparison Operators

Symbol	Mnemonic Equivalent	Definition	Example
=	EQ	equal to	a=3
^=	NE	not equal to	ane 3
¬=	NE	not equal to	
~=	NE	not equal to	
>	GT	greater than	num>5
<	LT	less than	num<8
>=	GE	greater than or equal to	sales> = 300
<=	LE	less than or equal to	sales< = 100
	IN	equal to one of a list	num in (3, 4, 5)

Source: SAS Institute Inc. 2013. *SAS(R) 9.4 Language Reference: Concepts, Second Edition.* Cary, NC: SAS Institute Inc.

to create similar values. When a function is used, contributing arguments with a missing value are ignored. Again consider the Sashelp dataset 'Shoes'. In order to determine total from sales and inventory, we can use one of two methods as depicted in Example 3.15.

TABLE 3.2. SAS Arithmetic Operator Table.

Arithmetic Operators

Symbol	Definition	Example	Result
**	exponentiation	a**3	raise A to the third power
*	multiplication	2*y	multiply 2 by the value of Y
/	division	var/5	divide the value of VAR by 5
+	addition	num+3	add 3 to the value of NUM
-	subtraction	sale-discount	subtract the value of DISCOUNT from the value of SALE

Source: SAS Institute Inc. 2013. *SAS(R) 9.4 Language Reference: Concepts, Second Edition.* Cary, NC: SAS Institute Inc.

	Sales	Inventory	Returns	sumtotal	plustotal
1	$29,761	$191,821	$769	221582	221582
2	$67,242	$118,036	$2,284	185278	185278
3	$76,793	$136,273	$2,433	213066	213066
4	$62,819	$204,284	$1,861	267103	267103
5	$68,641	$279,795	$1,771	348436	348436
6	$1,690	$16,634	$79	18324	18324

VIEWTABLE: Work.Y

FIGURE **3.8. Dataset Showing New Numeric Variables Sumtotal and Plustotal.**

EXAMPLE **3.15. Syntax for the SUM Function and the Corresponding Arithmetic Operator '+.'**

```
data y;
set sashelp.shoes;
sumtotal = sum (sales,inventory);
plustotal = sales + inventory;
run;
```

To clarify the difference between a SAS function and an arithmetic operator, let's assume that a few of the values for sales and inventory were missing (.) in the original dataset 'shoes' and take a look at the resulting values of sumtotal and plustotal in Figure 3.9.

Common measures such as maximum, minimum, and mean (average) values can also be calculated for numeric variables. Although there are a few ways to accomplish this, the most flexible way is to use a function. Consider the Sashelp dataset 'Shoes'. By creating new numeric variables using the MIN, MAX, and MEAN functions we can determine the minimum, maximum, and mean values of sales and inventory for each store. Example 3.16 shows sample syntax for creating these variables, and the resulting dataset can be found in Figure 3.10.

	Sales	Inventory	Returns	sumtotal	plustotal
1	$29,761	$191,821	$769	221582	221582
2	.	$118,036	$2,284	118036	.
3	$76,793	$136,273	$2,433	213066	213066
4	$62,819	.	$1,861	62819	.
5	$68,641	$279,795	$1,771	348436	348436
6	.	$16,634	$79	16634	.

VIEWTABLE: Work.H

FIGURE **3.9. Dataset Showing Result of Missing Values for Sales1 And Sales2.**

EXAMPLE **3.16. Syntax for Creating Numeric Variables Using MIN, MAX, and MEAN Functions.**

```
data x;
set sashelp.shoes;
mintoal = min (sales,inventory);
maxtotal = max (sales,inventory);
meantotal = mean (sales,inventory);
run;
```

	Sales	Inventory	Returns	mintoal	maxtotal	meantotal
1	$29,761	$191,821	$769	29761	191821	110791
2	$67,242	$118,036	$2,284	67242	118036	92639
3	$76,793	$136,273	$2,433	76793	136273	106533
4	$62,819	$204,284	$1,861	62819	204284	133551.5
5	$68,641	$279,795	$1,771	68641	279795	174218
6	$1,690	$16,634	$79	1690	16634	9162

VIEWTABLE: Work.X

FIGURE **3.10. Dataset Showing New Numeric Variables Minsales, Maxsales, and Meansales.**

Character Variables

Character variables can often present their own special challenges; variables of this type must be called upon by their exact values. Character variables are case sensitive, and incorrect spelling can be a common error in simplistic programming. Let's look at an example.

Output 3.3 shows the Log Window so that we may observe the results of two different data steps. Remember from Chapter 1 that the Log shows both sides of the conversation between SAS and the programmer. Syntax entered by the programmer is shown in black and SAS responds in colored font. In the first data step, the programmer requests all observations where the variable 'Region' is equal to "Afric". SAS uses the log to tell us that there are no observations with this value for 'Region'. In the next data step the programmer requests observations where 'Region' is equal to "Africa", and SAS reveals that there are 56 such observations. SAS cannot correctly identify the observations we are looking for unless we request character variable values exactly as they appear in the dataset.

OUTPUT 3.3. SAS Log Message When Variable Value Is Not Recognized due to Spelling Error.

```
105   Data spelling_error;
106   set sashelp.shoes;
107   where Region = "Afric";
108   run;

NOTE: There were 0 observations read from the data set SASHELP.SHOES.
      WHERE Region='Afric';
NOTE: The data set WORK.SPELLING_ERROR has 0 observations and 7 variables.
NOTE: DATA statement used (Total process time):
      real time           0.01 seconds
      cpu time            0.01 seconds


109
110   Data correct_spelling;
111   set sashelp.shoes;
112   where Region = "Africa";
113   run;

NOTE: There were 56 observations read from the data set SASHELP.SHOES.
      WHERE Region='Africa';
NOTE: The data set WORK.CORRECT_SPELLING has 56 observations and 7 variables.
NOTE: DATA statement used (Total process time):
      real time           0.00 seconds
      cpu time            0.00 seconds
```

Combining and Separating Variables

Other common variable tasks include concatenating two variables to create a composite variable or separating a composite variable into its original parts.

SAS functions can be used to combine two numeric variables. In the sashelp dataset 'Class' there are separate variables for 'age' and 'weight'. In order to create a unique identifier for each observation we can combine both of these variables. To accomplish this task SAS offers the CATS function (Example 3.17). The function takes two variables (removing any leading or trailing blanks) and puts them side by side returning a single character variable. To return it to a numeric format we can use an arithmetic operation (*1). The use of multiplication to convert a variable from character to numeric format is a useful trick for programmers.

EXAMPLE 3.17. Data Step Syntax for Concatenating Two Numeric Variables.
```
data cats function;
set sashelp.class;
new_variable = cats (age,weight);
HW = new_variable*1;
run;
```

To separate a single character variable into two unique variables, the substring function is used (Example 3.18). Specify the variable name and on the other side of the equal sign, invoke the function by typing 'substr', and then in parentheses indicate the original variable name, starting position (from the left) of the first character to be returned, followed by the total number of characters to be returned by the SUBSTR function. The new variables in the dataset 'separate' will appear exactly the same as in the original 'Class' dataset; age_separate as age and weight_separate as weight.

EXAMPLE 3.18. Data Step Syntax for Separating Character Variables.
```
data separate;
set cats function;
age_separate = substr (new_variable,1,2);
weight_separate = substr (new_variable,3,7);
run;
```

FIGURE 3.11. Example Data for Character Variables.

Often character variables are either packed full of information and squeezed into a tiny little living space or spread so far apart that only by putting them together can we make sense of their meaning. Address variables often create these types of issues: city and state as one variable is less flexible than the information split into two. In contrast, when variables like street number and street name are obtained as separate pieces of information, it makes more sense to put them together to create one useful variable. Issues like this can be dealt with using operators such as double vertical bars (||) and the sub-string function. Mock data in Figure 3.11 contains town and state variables separate (character1) and combined (character2).

In order to create one character variable from two character variables, a new variable must be created within the data step (Example 3.19). The new variable 'together' will appear as "WareMA". If it is necessary to include a comma or any other separator, that can be enclosed in single quotes and added as well. The variable 'with_comma' will appear as "Ware, MA". The CATS function can be used in the case of character variables as well (Example 3.20).

EXAMPLE 3.19. Data Step Syntax for Concatenating Character Variables Using Double Bars.

```
data put_together;
set character1 ;
together = town||state ;
with_comma = town|| ',' || state;
run;
```

EXAMPLE 3.20. Data Step Syntax for Concatenating Character Variables Using the CATS Function.

```
data put_together2;
set character1;
together = cats (town,state) ;
with_comma = cats (town,',',state);
run; run;
```

SAS provides a seemingly unending supply of functions that can be used to create variables of all kinds. For the purposes of this book we will not go any further than those functions previously described.

TEST YOUR SKILLS

Use the dataset created in Figure 3.2 and the techniques described in this chapter to accomplish the following tasks.

3.1 Add the variables Weight and Height to the dataset so that the resulting dataset looks like this:

ID	DOB	Weight__Pounds_	Height__inches_
1	08/26/1982	115	60
2	02/09/1982	110	62
3	10/12/2012	135	65
4	06/12/1954	200	70
5	01/18/1948	250	74
6	12/22/1945	225	72
7	10/24/1969	101	.
8	06/16/1972	155	68
9	04/01/1979	270	.
10	04/21/1948	180	68

3.2 Create the variable BMI (Body Mass Index) using the standard BMI calculation:

$$BMI = (Weight\_Pounds\_/(Height\_inches\_ * Height\_inches\_)) * 703$$

3.3 Create a categorical variable for BMI according to the standard guidelines:

BMI Range	Category
18–24.9	Healthy Weight
25–29.9	Overweight
30+	Obese

3.4 Create a subset of observations with only non-missing values for BMI.

SOLUTIONS

3.1 Add the variables Weight and Height to the dataset.

```
data BMI1_10;
input ID Weight_Pounds_ Height_inches_;
datalines;
 1 115 60
 2 110 62
 3 135 65
 4 200 70
 5 250 74
 6 225 72
 7 101 .
 8 155 68
 9 270 .
 10 180 68
 ;
run;

proc sort data = people1_10; by id; run;
proc sort data = bmi1_10; by id; run;
data dob_bmi;
merge people1_10 bmi1_10;
by ID;
run;
```

3.2 Create the variable BMI (Body Mass Index) using the standard BMI calculation.

```
data bmi2;
set dob_bmi;
BMI = (Weight_Pounds_/(Height_inches_*Height_inches_))
        *703; run;
```

	ID	DOB	Weight_Pounds_	Height_inches_	BMI
1	1	8273	115	60	22.456944444
2	2	8075	110	62	20.117065557
3	3	19278	135	65	22.462721893
4	4	-2029	200	70	28.693877551
5	5	-4366	250	74	32.094594595
6	6	-5123	225	72	30.512152778
7	7	3584	101		
8	8	4550	155	68	23.565095156
9	9	7030	270		
10	10	-4272	180	68	27.365916955

3.3 Create a categorical variable for BMI according to the standard guide-lines.

```
data bmi3;
set bmi2;
if 18<bmi<25 then bmi_cat = 'healthy weight';
else if 25<= bmi < 30 then bmi_cat = 'overweight';
else if 30 <= bmi then bmi_cat = 'obese';
run;
```

	ID	DOB	Weight_Pounds_	Height_inches_	BMI	bmi_cat
1	1	8273	115	60	22.456944444	healthy weight
2	2	8075	110	62	20.117065557	healthy weight
3	3	19278	135	65	22.462721893	healthy weight
4	4	-2029	200	70	28.693877551	overweight
5	5	-4366	250	74	32.094594595	obese
6	6	-5123	225	72	30.512152778	obese
7	7	3584	101			
8	8	4550	155	68	23.565095156	healthy weight
9	9	7030	270			
10	10	-4272	180	68	27.365916955	overweight

3.4 Create a subset of observations with only non-missing values for BMI.

```
data bmi_nonmissing;
set bmi3;
where bmi ne.;
run;
```

	ID	DOB	Weight_Pounds	Height_inches_	BMI	bmi_cat
1	1	8273	115	60	22.456944444	healthy weight
2	2	8075	110	62	20.117065557	healthy weight
3	3	19278	135	65	22.462721893	healthy weight
4	4	-2029	200	70	28.693877551	overweight
5	5	-4366	250	74	32.094594595	obese
6	6	-5123	225	72	30.512152778	obese
7	8	4550	155	68	23.565095156	healthy weight
8	10	-4272	180	68	27.365916955	overweight

CHAPTER 4

Advanced Concepts in Dataset and Variable Manipulation

This chapter focuses on some advanced topics in dataset and variable manipulation. We begin with a discussion of common errors that arise when combining datasets and then move on to some advanced topics in variable creation. As we execute more complex tasks, the challenges become more dynamic. In this chapter we discuss more sophisticated topics including merge errors, calendar dates, DO groups and loops, and ARRAYs. The examples included in this section are by no means all inclusive, but rather are intended to cover some common issues that come up when the concepts introduced up to this point are employed in the real world.

MERGE ERRORS

While merging datasets is a useful and commonly employed technique, it is not always straightforward. There are many ways that a data merge can result in errant data; here we focus on two of the most common issues.

When merging two or more datasets, SAS requires that variables listed in the BY statement be found in all of the datasets to be merged. Further, SAS requires that these BY variables have identical characteristics in each dataset. Consider again the datasets 'people1_10' and 'people11_20'; in the case where the variable ID has more than one length, as defined in Chapter 2, SAS warns that the merge may result in errant data (Output 4.1). Although this will not stop the merge, it could create an inaccurate dataset.

OUTPUT 4.1. Log Message for a Merge Error.

```
WARNING: Multiple lengths were specified for the BY variable ID by input data sets. This may cause
         unexpected results.
NOTE: There were 10 observations read from the data set WORK.PEOPLE11_20.
NOTE: There were 10 observations read from the data set MH.PEOPLE1_10.
NOTE: The data set WORK.PEOPLE1_20 has 20 observations and 2 variables.
NOTE: DATA statement used (Total process time):
      real time           0.00 seconds
      cpu time            0.00 seconds
```

Another common issue when merging datasets is the overwriting of variables with the same name. If a variable of the same name exists in each of the datasets being merged, the resulting dataset will have only one variable with that name and no indication of which dataset the values were taken from. Additionally, issues with respect to variable characteristics, similar to the length complication previously described in this section, can arise when merging datasets with the same variable in more than one dataset. Therefore, it is wise to be sure that each variable not listed in the BY statement has a unique name in each dataset. This will prevent variables from being unintentionally overwritten during the merge process.

CALENDAR DATES IN SAS

Dates are frequently used to describe the date that data was collected, the date that a relevant event occurred, or the date that data were entered into the dataset. In order to maximize the functionality of stored dates, SAS stores dates numerically. The date January 1, 1960 is represented by the number zero, January 2, 1960 is represented by the number 1, and so on and so forth. Dates before January 1, 1960 are assigned the appropriate negative number; in other words, December 31, 1959 is stored as -1.

Keeping in mind this SAS date storage convention, it is easy to imagine that most of the dates we encounter on a regular basis are five-digit numbers. In order to read these dates in the real world, we use formats. In general, formats change the appearance of a variable without changing its content. Variables can be formatted in two ways: using a FORMAT statement or creating a new variable. One commonly used format is MMDDYY8. Using this format, the date January 1, 1960 (stored by SAS as 0) would be displayed as 01/01/60. In the syntax below (Example 4.1) the new variable 'Date' and the formatted variable 'Rawdate' are assigned the same format and would therefore appear the same in a dataset.

EXAMPLE 4.1. Syntax for Creating and Formatting Date Variables.

```
DATE = INPUT (RAWDATE, MMDDYY8.) ;
FORMAT RAWDATE MMDDYY8.;
```

When values are stored internally as SAS dates, they can be called upon in syntax using the following technique: a two-digit day of the month, followed by the first three letters of the calendar month, followed by a four-digit year, all enclosed in matching quotes immediately followed by the letter "D." For instance, if we wanted to subset our data by creating a dataset with all observations dated after June 1, 2013, we would use the syntax in Example 4.2.

EXAMPLE 4.2. Syntax for Subsetting Data Using a Specified Date.

```
DATA X;
SET LIBRARY.DATA;
WHERE DATE > '01JUN2013'D;
RUN;
```

Common date-related tasks are (1) to create a date when month, day, and year are stored separately; and (2) to extract a piece of the date from an existing variable. Both of these tasks are accomplished using functions to create new variables. In Example 4.3 we use the MDY function to create a date from three numeric variables: 'month,' 'day,' and 'year.' In Example 4.4 the MONTH function is used to extract the month from a complete date. The DAY and YEAR functions are executed in a parallel manner.

EXAMPLE 4.3. Syntax for the MDY Function.

```
DATE = MDY(MONTH,DAY,YEAR) ;
```

EXAMPLE 4.4. Syntax for the MONTH Function.

```
MONTH = MONTH (DATE) ;
```

In order to reference the current date, the programmer can use either of the two functions that will return today's date: TODAY () or DATE (). For instance, the syntax in Example 4.5 calculates current age (in years) based on the date of birth.

EXAMPLE 4.5. Syntax for the TODAY() Function.
```
AGE = (TODAY()- DATE_OF_BIRTH)/ 365.25;
```

In this example we divide the number of days by 365.25 to calculate the participant's age in years (365 days in a year, plus 0.25 to account for leap years).

Often a date is linked with a time. In these cases, SAS can store the data as one variable or two. Time is measured as the number of seconds from midnight on the associated date and takes on values of 0–86,400. When date and time are stored as one value, the value is measured as the number of seconds between January 1, 1960 and the specified time on the specified date. Conventions for tasks similar to those outlined previously with respect to date are provided in Example 4.6.

EXAMPLE 4.6. Syntax for Selected Date and Time Functions.
```
DATE_WITH_TIME = DATETIME (DATE, TIME);
DATE_ONLY = DATEPART (DATE_WITH_TIME);
TIME_ONLY = TIMEPART (DATE_WITH_TIME);
FORMAT TIME_ONLY TIMEAMPM.;
```

The first line describes the creation of a datetime variable from the date and time pieces. The second and third lines illustrate how to extract the date and time pieces, respectively, and the fourth line shows a common time format TIMEAMPM, which will show the value as HH:MM:SS:AM/PM.

For a more in-depth discussion of SAS dates and times, we recommend *The Essential Guide to SAS Dates and Times* by Derek P. Morgan (2006).

DO GROUPS AND LOOPS AND VARIABLE ARRAYS

When cleaning a dataset, programmers often find the need to perform a set of tasks on only those variables that meet specific criteria and/or perform the same task on multiple variables. While this can be accomplished by repeating simple syntax over and over in a data step, it can be accomplished more efficiently by using DO groups and loops or variable ARRAYs. In this section we provide an overview of when and how these powerful SAS tools can be used.

DO groups are often used in the data step in conjunction with IF/THEN statements (Example 3.14) in order to perform multiple tasks on observations that meet specified criteria. DO groups and loops always begin with a DO statement and are closed with an END statement. In Example 4.7, separate syntax is executed depending on whether the variable sex indicates that the observation reflects a male or female individual. Male individuals are identified using an IF statement and then assigned the value '1' for gender and the value 'blue' for color in a DO group. Similarly, female individuals are assigned the values '2' and 'pink', respectively.

EXAMPLE **4.7. Syntax for a DO Group.**

```
data do_group;
set sashelp.class;
if sex = 'M' then do;
    gender = 1;
    color = 'blue';
    end;
else if sex = 'F' then do;
    gender = 2;
    color = 'pink';
    end;
run;
```

The DO group described in Example 4.7 allows the programmer to execute multiple tasks on observations that meet specific criteria. Using an ARRAY allows the programmer to perform tasks on a group or groups of variables. Frequently, DO loops and ARRAYs are used together in order to accomplish a complex programming task in the most efficient manner. Consider the syntax in Example 4.8. First, an ARRAY statement names a group of variables "decimal" and specifies which variables are included (height and weight). DO OVER (a special type of DO loop) is used to perform the CEIL function on all variables specified in the "decimal" array.

	Name	Sex	Age	Height	Weight	gender	color
1	Alfred	M	14	69	112.5	1	blue
2	Alice	F	13	56.5	84	2	pink
3	Barbara	F	13	65.3	98	2	pink
4	Carol	F	14	62.8	102.5	2	pink
5	Henry	M	14	63.5	102.5	1	blue
6	James	M	12	57.3	83	1	blue
7	Jane	F	12	59.8	84.5	2	pink
8	Janet	F	15	62.5	112.5	2	pink
9	Jeffrey	M	13	62.5	84	1	blue
10	John	M	12	59	99.5	1	blue
11	Joyce	F	11	51.3	50.5	2	pink
12	Judy	F	14	64.3	90	2	pink
13	Louise	F	12	56.3	77	2	pink
14	Mary	F	15	66.5	112	2	pink
15	Philip	M	16	72	150	1	blue
16	Robert	M	12	64.8	128	1	blue
17	Ronald	M	15	67	133	1	blue
18	Thomas	M	11	57.5	85	1	blue
19	William	M	15	66.5	112	1	blue

FIGURE 4.1. Resulting Dataset of DO Group Syntax.

EXAMPLE 4.8. Syntax for DO OVER Statement.

```
data class;
set sashelp.class;
array decimal height weight;
do over decimal;
        decimal = ceil(decimal);
end;
run;
```

Creating a new group of variables based on a preexisting group of variables provides another good example of DO loops and ARRAYs being used together. Consider the Sashelp dataset 'cars' and suppose that we wish to create a new set of variables where the continuous variables "msrp" and "invoice" are categorized at $25,000 increments. The syntax in Example 4.9 is the long and repetitive approach to creating two new variables. Example 4.10 shows how the task can be more efficiently accomplished using two arrays. In this example, the arrays are 'indexed,' which means that the number of variables is specified in the ARRAY statement. Indexing the array allows the programmer to reference and use the order of the variables to accomplish tasks. In this

VIEWTABLE: Sashelp.Class (Student Data)				
	Name	Sex	Age	Height	Weight
1	Alfred	M	14	69	112.5
2	Alice	F	13	56.5	84
3	Barbara	F	13	65.3	98
4	Carol	F	14	62.8	102.5
5	Henry	M	14	63.5	102.5
6	James	M	12	57.3	83
7	Jane	F	12	59.8	84.5
8	Janet	F	15	62.5	112.5
9	Jeffrey	M	13	62.5	84
10	John	M	12	59	99.5
11	Joyce	F	11	51.3	50.5
12	Judy	F	14	64.3	90
13	Louise	F	12	56.3	77
14	Mary	F	15	66.5	112
15	Philip	M	16	72	150
16	Robert	M	12	64.8	128
17	Ronald	M	15	67	133
18	Thomas	M	11	57.5	85
19	William	M	15	66.5	112

VIEWTABLE: Work.Class				
	Name	Sex	Age	Height	Weight
1	Alfred	M	14	69	113
2	Alice	F	13	57	84
3	Barbara	F	13	66	98
4	Carol	F	14	63	103
5	Henry	M	14	64	103
6	James	M	12	58	83
7	Jane	F	12	60	85
8	Janet	F	15	63	113
9	Jeffrey	M	13	63	84
10	John	M	12	59	100
11	Joyce	F	11	52	51
12	Judy	F	14	65	90
13	Louise	F	12	57	77
14	Mary	F	15	67	112
15	Philip	M	16	72	150
16	Robert	M	12	65	128
17	Ronald	M	15	67	133
18	Thomas	M	11	58	85
19	William	M	15	67	112

FIGURE 4.2. Dataset Resulting from DO OVER Syntax.

case, the first variable in the "dollar" array is used to create the first variable in the "dollar_cat" array.

EXAMPLE 4.9. Data Step Syntax to Create Variables without ARRAYs or DO Loops.

```
data cars;
set sashelp.cars;

if msrp < 25000 then msrp_cat = 1;
else if 25000<= msrp < 50000 then msrp_cat = 2;
else if 50000<= msrp < 75000 then msrp_cat = 3;
else if 75000<= msrp < 100000 then msrp_cat = 4;
else if 100000<= msrp < 125000 then msrp_cat = 5;
else if 125000<= msrp < 150000 then msrp_cat = 6;
else if 150000<= msrp < 175000 then msrp_cat = 7;
else if 175000<= msrp < 200000 then msrp_cat = 8;

if invoice < 25000 then invoice_cat = 1;
else if 25000<= invoice < 50000 then invoice_cat = 2;
else if 50000<= invoice < 75000 then invoice_cat = 3;
else if 75000<= invoice < 100000 then invoice_cat = 4;
else if 100000<= invoice < 125000 then invoice_cat = 5;
else if 125000<= invoice < 150000 then invoice_cat = 6;
else if 150000<= invoice < 175000 then invoice_cat = 7;
else if 175000<= invoice < 200000 then invoice_cat = 8;

run;
```

VIEWTABLE: WorkCars	msrp_cat	invoice_cat
1	2	2
2	1	1
3	2	1
4	2	2
5	2	2
6	2	2
7	4	4
8	2	1
9	2	2
10	2	2

VIEWTABLE: WorkCars2	msrp_cat_array	invoice_cat_array
1	2	2
2	1	1
3	2	1
4	2	2
5	2	2
6	2	2
7	4	4
8	2	1
9	2	2
10	2	2

FIGURE 4.3. Dataset Results of Creating Categorical Variables.

EXAMPLE 4.10. Data Step Syntax to Create Variables with ARRAYs and DO Loops.

```
data cars2;
set sashelp.cars;
array dollar (2) msrp invoice;
array dollar_cat (2) msrp_cat_array invoice_cat_array;

DO I = 1 to 2;
if dollar (i)< 25000 then dollar_cat (i) = 1;
else if 25000<= dollar (i) < 50000 then dollar_cat (i) = 2;
else if 50000<= dollar (i)< 75000 then dollar_cat (i) = 3;
else if 75000<= dollar (i)< 100000 then dollar_cat (i) = 4;
else if 100000<= dollar (i) < 125000 then dollar_cat (i) = 5;
else if 125000<= dollar (i)< 150000 then dollar_cat (i) = 6;
else if 150000<= dollar (i)< 175000 then dollar_cat (i) = 7;
else if 175000<= dollar (i)< 200000 then dollar_cat (i) = 8;
end;
run;
```

TEST YOUR SKILLS

Using the dataset people1_10 created in Chapter 3 and the techniques described in this chapter, accomplish the following tasks:

4.1 Create a new dataset to include only those with a date of birth after January 1, 1982 AND format the variable DOB as a calendar date.

4.2 Create the variable "Age" for each observation in the dataset poeple1_10.

Using the sashelp dataset 'cars', accomplish the following task:

4.3 Use a DO Loop and ARRAY (as shown in Example 4.10) to recreate the categorical variables 'msrp_cat_array' and 'invoice_cat_array' with three categories: $0.00 – $75,000.00, $75,000.01 – $150,000.00, and $150,000.01 – $200,000.00.

SOLUTIONS

4.1 Create a new dataset to include only those with a date of birth after January 1, 1982 AND format the variable DOB as a calendar date.

```
data dobsubset;
set people1_10;
where dob > '01jan1982'd;
FORMAT DOB MMDDYY8.; run;
```

	ID	DOB
1	1	08/26/82
2	2	02/09/82
3	3	10/12/12

4.2 Create the variable "Age" for each observation in the dataset people1_10.

```
data age;
set people1_10;
age = (TODAY()- DOB)/ 365.25;
RUN;
```

	ID	DOB	age
1	1	8273	32.580424367
2	2	8075	33.122518823
3	3	19278	2.4503764545
4	4	-2029	60.785763176
5	5	-4366	67.184120465
6	6	-5123	69.256673511
7	7	3584	45.418206708
8	8	4550	42.773442847
9	9	7030	35.983572895
10	10	-4272	66.926762491

4.3 Use a DO Loop and Array (as shown in Example 4.10) to recreate the categorical variables 'msrp_cat_array' and 'invoice_cat_array' with three categories: $0.00 – $75,000.00, $75,000.01 – $150,000.00, and $150,000.01 – $200,000.00.

```
data cars3;
set sashelp.cars;
array dollar (2) msrp invoice;
array dollar_cat (2) msrp_cat_array invoice_cat_array;

DO I = 1 to 2;
if 0 < dollar (i)< 75000 then dollar_cat (i) = 1;
else if 75000<= dollar (i) < 150000 then dollar_cat
(i) = 2;
else if 150000<= dollar (i)< 200000 then dollar_cat
(i) = 3;
end;
run;
```

CHAPTER 5

Introduction to Common Procedures

Once a dataset has been created and stored in SAS, the choices are limitless. Most tasks are completed using SAS-defined procedures, often referred to as PROCs. Each PROC allows the user to manipulate and/or view their data in a new way. SAS offers a variety of different procedures; within each one, a number of options can be employed, allowing the user ultimate flexibility in their final product. Two common procedures are described in this chapter, the SORT procedure and the PRINT procedure, presented along with some of their most useful options.

THE SORT PROCEDURE

What It Does and How It Works

PROC SORT orders a SAS dataset according to the value of the variable that is listed in the BY statement. This procedure is a prerequisite for invoking a BY statement in any subsequent data steps or procedures. For syntax to run properly, the data must be sorted by the variables listed in the BY statement. Datasets can be sorted by multiple variables to further specify the order of

	ID			ID
1	2	1		1
2	4	2		2
3	4	3		4
4	5	4		4
5	6	5		5
6	7	6		6
7	8	7		7
8	9	8		8
9	1	9		9

FIGURE 5.1. Unsorted versus Sorted Datasets.

observations. When a PROC SORT is performed, the variable(s) specified in the BY statement will be placed in ascending order. For example, the dataset featured on the left-hand side of Figure 5.1 is unsorted, and on the right it is sorted. The sorted view displays all observations with the smallest value of 'id' first, followed by all other observations in ascending numerical order.

Let's try an example. First, open the sashelp dataset 'Class.' Notice that there are 5 variables and 19 observations. By visually assessing the data we can see that it is sorted alphabetically by name. Let's assume that for our analysis it is more appropriate to sort this information by age. Example 5.1 provides syntax for changing the location and name of the existing sashelp dataset 'Class' and then sorting the new dataset 'SortAge' by the single variable 'age.' Enter the syntax in the editor window and click the running person icon.

EXAMPLE 5.1. Syntax for Sorting by One Variable Using PROC SORT.

```
data SortAge;
set sashelp.class;
run;

proc sort data = SortAge; by age; run;
```

When opened in the Viewtable, the observations in this dataset (SortAge) should now be in ascending order according to their value in the variable age. It is important to remember that the SORT procedure permanently changes the order of a dataset. When working with original data files, it is good practice to create a new dataset and then proceed to manipulating the data.

Example 5.2 provides sample syntax for sorting by two variables, age and height, in the dataset 'SortAge'. After executing the syntax, notice that the dataset is first sorted by age, with the smallest value first, and values in the height variable are sorted second. If the BY variable included character values, the observations would be sorted in alphabetical order.

EXAMPLE 5.2. **Syntax for Sorting by Two Variables Using PROC SORT.**

```
proc sort data = SortAge;
by age height;
run;
```

In Chapter 2, Figure 2.6 displays the output of a basic contents procedure with sort order equal to 'yes'. When a PROC CONTENTS is executed on the sorted dataset 'SortAge', the output information is similar (Figure 5.2). *Sorted* indicates 'yes', and included at the end of the output is a new box labeled 'Sort Information'. Sorted by includes the variable names in which the dataset is sorted. Validated confirms that the data is in fact sorted.

The SAS System

The CONTENTS Procedure

Data Set Name	WORK.SORTAGE	Observations	19
Member Type	DATA	Variables	5
Engine	V9	Indexes	0
Created	11/03/2014 14:22:43	Observation Length	40
Last Modified	11/03/2014 14:22:43	Deleted Observations	0
Protection		Compressed	NO
Data Set Type		Sorted	YES
Label			
Data Representation	WINDOWS_64		
Encoding	wlatin1 Western (Windows)		

Sort Information	
Sortedby	Age
Validated	YES
Character Set	ANSI

FIGURE 5.2. CONTENTS Procedure Output Indicating Sort Order.

More Uses for the SORT Procedure

When a BY statement is included in a data step or a procedure, the data must be sorted according to the variable specified in the BY statement. In Chapter 3, Example 3.7 utilizes the SORT procedure prior to merging two datasets; the datasets were merged 'by id', therefore both datasets needed to be sorted by the variable 'id' before the merge could be executed. In a procedure, the same holds true; if the procedure includes a BY statement, but the data is not sorted, then SAS will only include results on the observations for the first group from which it reads observations. When this type of error occurs, SAS provides an ERROR message in the Log (Output 5.1). If this occurs, the Results Viewer may still show output but it will not be accurate. This is a great example of why checking the Log is so important.

OUTPUT 5.1. SAS Log Error Message for Unsorted Data.

```
43    proc print data = SortAge; by sex; run;

ERROR: Data set WORK.SORTAGE is not sorted in ascending sequence. The current BY group has Sex
       = M and the next BY group has Sex = F.
NOTE: The SAS System stopped processing this step because of errors.
NOTE: There were 4 observations read from the data set WORK.SORTAGE.
NOTE: PROCEDURE PRINT used (Total process time):
      real time           0.21 seconds
      cpu time            0.01 seconds
```

A DATA step often needs to include a BY statement to indicate in what order SAS should navigate through the dataset. Consider our dataset 'SortAge'. Let's say that the only information we need to report is on the first age of each gender.

EXAMPLE 5.3 Incomplete Syntax for Subsetting Only the First Listing of the BY Variable.

```
data first_type;
set SortAge;
by sex;
if first.sex;
run;
```

Running the syntax in Example 5.3 is one way of requesting that information. The log will indicate that the dataset first_type may be incomplete because the BY variables are not properly sorted in the dataset 'SortAge'. To correct this issue, include a PROC SORT . prior to the data statement (Example 5.4).

EXAMPLE 5.4. Complete Syntax for Subsetting the First Observation for Each Value of the BY Variable.

```
proc sort data = SortAge; by sex; run;
data first_type;
set SortAge;
by sex;
if first.sex;
run;
```

Figure 5.3 is the result of the complete syntax in Example 5.4. The dataset 'First_type' includes two observations: the youngest male and female in the Sashelp dataset 'Class.'

	Name	Sex	Age	Height	Weight
1	Joyce	F	11	51.3	50.5
2	Thomas	M	11	57.5	85

FIGURE **5.3. Resulting Dataset for Syntax in Example 5.4.**

Duplicate Observations

According to Wikipedia, the definition of 'duplicate' is "Data redundancy, either wanted or unwanted."[1] Duplicates are, usually, unwanted pieces of information that can sneak in during any point of data collection. When dealing with duplicates, it is crucial to identify their existence and equally important to determine their origin. Fieldwork, manual entry of information, merging, setting and use of inappropriate datasets can all result in the inadvertent creation of duplicates.

The sort procedure can be used to find and output information about duplicate observations, using the NODUP and NODUPKEY options. Using NODUP will automatically delete an observation if it contains exactly the same values *for all variables* in another observation. This record will no longer appear in the dataset and is permanently deleted. Including the NODUPKEY option will result in deletion of observations only if variable values are an exact match to the value of the BY variable. Observations that match on other variables not specified in the BY statement will not be deleted. Successful

[1] http://en.wikipedia.org/wiki/Duplicate

execution of the NODUP and NODUPKEY options is contingent on proper use of the BY variable.

Example 5.5 sorts the dataset 'SortAge' by the variable age. Since the NODUP option is employed, SAS will scan across all variables for each observation looking for exact matches on all variable values. The log (Output 5.2) indicates that of the 19 observations in 'SortAge' there were zero duplicate observations. Figure 5.4 shows that the dataset 'SortAge' is now sorted by age.

EXAMPLE 5.5. SORT Procedure Syntax for the NODUP Option.

```
proc sort data = SortAge nodup;
by age;
run;
```

OUTPUT 5.2. Log Note for the NODUP Option.

```
NOTE: There were 19 observations read from the data set WORK.SORTAGE.
NOTE: 0 duplicate observations were deleted.
NOTE: The data set WORK.SORTAGE has 19 observations and 5 variables.
NOTE: PROCEDURE SORT used (Total process time):
      real time              0.01 seconds
      cpu time               0.01 seconds
```

	Name	Sex	Age	Height	Weight
1	Joyce	F	11	51.3	50.5
2	Thomas	M	11	57.5	85
3	James	M	12	57.3	83
4	Jane	F	12	59.8	84.5
5	John	M	12	59	99.5
6	Louise	F	12	56.3	77
7	Robert	M	12	64.8	128
8	Alice	F	13	56.5	84
9	Barbara	F	13	65.3	98
10	Jeffrey	M	13	62.5	84
11	Alfred	M	14	69	112.5
12	Carol	F	14	62.8	102.5
13	Henry	M	14	63.5	102.5
14	Judy	F	14	64.3	90
15	Janet	F	15	62.5	112.5
16	Mary	F	15	66.5	112
17	Ronald	M	15	67	133
18	William	M	15	66.5	112
19	Philip	M	16	72	150

FIGURE 5.4. Dataset Sorted by Age, No Exact Duplicates.

In Example 5.6, the NODUPKEY option requests that while SAS sorts the dataset 'SortAge' by the variable age, it deletes all preceding observations that have a duplicate value for the variable age. The Log (Output 5.3) indicates that of the 19 observations, 13 were excluded due to duplicate key values; the resulting dataset (Figure 5.5) now only includes 6 observations. Remember, the dataset 'SortAge' has been permanently changed.

EXAMPLE 5.6. Syntax for the NODUPKEY Option in the SORT Procedure.

```
proc sort data = SortAge nodupkey;
by age;
run;
```

OUTPUT 5.3. Log Note for the NODUPKEY Option.

```
NOTE: There were 19 observations read from the data set WORK.SORTAGE.
NOTE: 13 observations with duplicate key values were deleted.
NOTE: The data set WORK.SORTAGE has 6 observations and 5 variables.
NOTE: PROCEDURE SORT used (Total process time):
      real time          0.45 seconds
      cpu time           0.00 seconds
```

	Name	Sex	Age	Height	Weight
1	Joyce	F	11	51.3	50.5
2	James	M	12	57.3	83
3	Alice	F	13	56.5	84
4	Alfred	M	14	69	112.5
5	Janet	F	15	62.5	112.5
6	Philip	M	16	72	150

FIGURE 5.5. Dataset Sorted by Age with the NODUPKEY Option.

To conduct data cleaning efficiently, it is helpful to produce a list of the observations that have been excluded from a dataset due to duplicate values. To accomplish this task, SAS offers the DUPOUT option (Example 5.7).

EXAMPLE 5.7. SORT Procedure Syntax for the NODUPKEY and DUPOUT Options.

```
proc sort data = SortAge nodupkey dupout = check_duplicates;
by age;
run;
```

When executed, the syntax in Example 5.7 creates an additional dataset called 'check_duplicates', which we refer to as an output dataset. This dataset will appear in the work library and contains the deleted observations that had duplicate values of the variable age. This dataset can be useful during the investigation phase of data cleaning. Important information may include the values of associated variables: for example, if there is a date available, was the information duplicated in error or is this information valid but simply collected at a different time. Missing data may also be the cause of a duplicate observation, or may be a useful place to start when attempting to solve a duplicate mystery. The important thing to realize here is that the programmer has used a few standard SAS options to collect valuable information and eventually produce a clean and accurate dataset.

THE PRINT PROCEDURE

What It Does and How It Works

The PRINT procedure literally 'prints' the contents of the specified dataset in the Output and Results Viewer windows. From these windows, information can be printed directly on paper or copied and pasted into different software for reporting. In Chapter 8 we will discuss the SAS Output Delivery System (ODS) that allows the user to export output to other software. It does not allow the programmer to alter the dataset in any way, but it can be used to produce a printable view of a dataset or subset of data. Procedure options listed in Table 5.1 allow the user to alter the appearance of printed output. Options, such as titles, page orientation, and page number, can also be included but do not have to be part of the PRINT procedure.

The PRINT procedure is often used as a method for identifying and cleaning errant observations or as a way to see the contents of a particular variable or observation, without having to create a new dataset or open a cumbersome dataset in the Viewtable. For larger datasets, the PRINT procedure is a method for checking data on a more specified scale. For smaller datasets, the PRINT procedure can be used as a method for checking that syntax has been executed successfully.

For our discussion of PROC PRINT we will continue with our created dataset 'Sortage'. Go ahead and rerun the original syntax shown in Example 5.1 to ensure the dataset is complete. Our dataset 'sortage' contains

Obs	Name	Sex	Age	Height	Weight
1	Alfred	M	14	69.0	112.5
2	Alice	F	13	56.5	84.0
3	Barbara	F	13	65.3	98.0
4	Carol	F	14	62.8	102.5
5	Henry	M	14	63.5	102.5
6	James	M	12	57.3	83.0
7	Jane	F	12	59.8	84.5
8	Janet	F	15	62.5	112.5
9	Jeffrey	M	13	62.5	84.0
10	John	M	12	59.0	99.5
11	Joyce	F	11	51.3	50.5
12	Judy	F	14	64.3	90.0
13	Louise	F	12	56.3	77.0
14	Mary	F	15	66.5	112.0
15	Philip	M	16	72.0	150.0
16	Robert	M	12	64.8	128.0
17	Ronald	M	15	67.0	133.0
18	Thomas	M	11	57.5	85.0
19	William	M	15	66.5	112.0

FIGURE 5.6. PRINT Procedure Output from Example 5.8.

5 variables and 19 observations. Example 5.8 shows basic PRINT procedure syntax.

EXAMPLE 5.8. Default Syntax for the PRINT Procedure.

```
proc print data = sortage;
run;
```

Figure 5.6 shows the default format for the PRINT procedure as it appears in the results viewer. On the far left, the column 'obs' displays the observation number for each line of data. This is particularly useful in cases where there is no other unique identifier in the data, or when there are multiple columns of data, which forces more than one line of data per observation in the printed output. Each column represents a variable and is marked by the variable name at the top of each page of output. Data appears exactly as it is stored and formatted.

TABLE 5.1. PRINT Procedure Options and Additional Statements.	
Syntax	Result
Options:	
NOOBS	Removes the column of data providing the SAS assigned observation number
D	Double spaces the output
LABEL	Uses variable labels rather than variable names as column headings
Statements:	
ID	Specifies one or more variables to use instead of observation numbers to identify observations in the report
VAR	Specifies a subset of variables to appear in the output
WHERE	Subsets the input dataset and limits the output to those observations meeting the specified criteria
BY	Produces a separate section of the report for each BY group

Options and Statements

Options in the PROC PRINT statement allow the user to change the visual appearance of the output, and additional statements within the procedure allow the user to modify which observations and variables are displayed in the output. Table 5.1 lists some commonly used options and statements and describes their functions.

To employ options or statements from Table 5.1, they must be placed correctly in the syntax. The options (NOOBS, LABEL, and D) need to be included immediately after specifying the dataset name, whereas the statements (BY, ID, VAR, and WHERE) stand alone and require their own specific syntax structure.

Always, when writing syntax, it is important to let the colors from the enhanced editor be a guide; if the command does not turn blue, then it may be located in the incorrect place. When the syntax shown in Example 5.9 is entered into the enhanced editor, notice that the options/statements from Table 5.1 turn blue. This is a good indicator that we have correctly placed them within our program. When using BY in any procedure (or DATA step), remember to first sort the dataset by that variable. Failing to do this will create invalid output in the Results Viewer, and the Log will include an error stating that "the dataset is not sorted in ascending sequence."

The first set of syntax in Example 5.9 sorts the dataset 'sortage' by the variable age. This is how the data will be grouped in the output. The second portion of syntax is the actual PRINT procedure, including the options NOOBS and LABEL. In contrast to Figure 5.6, this syntax instructs SAS to exclude the observation number, and instead of the variable names, SAS will print the variable labels. Using an ID statement indicates what variable we would like to use to identify observations. Figure 5.7 is the result of running the syntax in Example 5.9. Grouped by age, the observations are listed by sex.

EXAMPLE 5.9. PRINT Procedure Syntax with NOOBS and LABEL Options.

```
proc sort data = sortage;
by age;
run;
proc print data = sortage noobs label;
by age;
id sex;
run;
```

Age=11

Sex	Name	Height	Weight
F	Joyce	51.3	50.5
M	Thomas	57.5	85.0

Age=12

Sex	Name	Height	Weight
M	James	57.3	83.0
F	Jane	59.8	84.5
M	John	59.0	99.5
F	Louise	56.3	77.0
M	Robert	64.8	128.0

Age=13

Sex	Name	Height	Weight
F	Alice	56.5	84
F	Barbara	65.3	98
M	Jeffrey	62.5	84

Age=14

Sex	Name	Height	Weight
M	Alfred	69.0	112.5
F	Carol	62.8	102.5
M	Henry	63.5	102.5
F	Judy	64.3	90.0

Age=15

Sex	Name	Height	Weight
F	Janet	62.5	112.5
F	Mary	66.5	112.0
M	Ronald	67.0	133.0
M	William	66.5	112.0

Age=16

Sex	Name	Height	Weight
M	Philip	72	150

FIGURE 5.7. Results Viewer Output of PROC PRINT with NOOBS and LABEL Options.

Titles are often essential when printing data for others to view and are easily included using a TITLE statement. Prior to the PROC statement, the title can be specified as displayed in Example 5.10. If more than one title is required, then multiple TITLE statements can be included (followed by numbers) to tell SAS in what order the titles should appear (Example 5.10). Text written in the TITLE statements will appear in the output exactly as it is written within the quotes.

EXAMPLE 5.10 Reporting Data with Proc Print

```
title1 'Title of Department;
title2 'Description of Data;
proc print data = sortage noobs label;
by age;
id sex;
run;
```

TEST YOUR SKILLS

The exercises in this section refer to the datasets created in previous Test Your Skills sections. Before you begin, identify the datasets you created in Exercises 3.2 and 4.2.

5.1 Combine the two datasets to create a new dataset with six variables:

> ID, DOB, Age, Height_inches_, Weight_pounds_, BMI.

5.2 Sort the dataset created in Exercise 5.1 by the variable age.

5.3 Use the print procedure to check for missing data.

5.4 Create a report to identify observations that need consideration later due to missing values.

5.5 Recreate the variable bmi_cat created in Exercise 3.3 and use the print procedure to check your work.

SOLUTIONS

5.1 Combine the two datasets to create a new dataset with six variables:

> ID, DOB, Age, Height_inches_, Weight_pounds_, BMI.

```
proc sort data = age; by id; run;
proc sort data = bmi2; by id; run;
data combine;
merge age bmi2;
by id;
format dob mmddyy8.;
run;
```

5.2 Sort the dataset created in Exercise 5.1 by the variable age.

```
proc sort data = combine; by age; run;
```

5.3 Use the print procedure to check for missing data.

```
proc print data = combine; run;
```

Obs	ID	DOB	age	Weight_Pounds_	Height_inches_	BMI
1	3	10/12/12	2.4504	135	65	22.4627
2	1	08/26/82	32.5804	115	60	22.4569
3	2	02/09/82	33.1225	110	62	20.1171
4	9	04/01/79	35.9836	270	.	.
5	8	06/16/72	42.7734	155	68	23.5651
6	7	10/24/69	45.4182	101	.	.
7	4	06/12/54	60.7858	200	70	28.6939
8	10	04/21/48	66.9268	180	68	27.3659
9	5	01/18/48	67.1841	250	74	32.0946
10	6	12/22/45	69.2567	225	72	30.5122

5.4 Create a report to identify observations that need consideration later due to missing values.

```
proc print data = combine;
where bmi =.;
run;
```

Obs	ID	DOB	age	Weight_Pounds_	Height_inches_	BMI
4	9	04/01/79	35.9836	270	.	.
6	7	10/24/69	45.4182	101	.	.

5.5 Recreate the variable bmi_cat created in Exercise 3.3 and use the print procedure to check your work.

```
data combine2;
set combine;
if 18<bmi<25 then bmi_cat = 'healthy weight';
else if 25<= bmi < 30 then bmi_cat = 'overweight';
else if 30 <= bmi then bmi_cat = 'obese';
run;
proc print data = combine2;
var bmi bmi_cat;
run;
```

Obs	BMI	bmi_cat
1	22.4627	healthy weight
2	22.4569	healthy weight
3	20.1171	healthy weight
4	.	
5	23.5651	healthy weight
6	.	
7	28.6939	overweight
8	27.3659	overweight
9	32.0946	obese
10	30.5122	obese

CHAPTER 6

Procedures for Simple Statistics

Most of the time, regular data reporting consists of simple statistics. Answers to questions like "how many?", "what proportion?", "what's the highest value?", and "are those variables related?" commonly form the basis of such reporting. SAS provides a selection of procedures that are best used to answer these most basic questions in a way that is accurate, succinct, and simple. In this chapter, we discuss four procedures that are commonly used to create user-friendly reports that answer these questions: FREQUENCY, MEANS, UNIVARIATE, and CORR.

THE FREQUENCY PROCEDURE

Perhaps the simplest way to answer the question "how many" is to use the FREQUENCY procedure, typically referred to as PROC FREQ. This procedure tells the user how many observations carry each value of a particular variable by producing tabular or list-style frequency counts for all variables listed in the TABLES statement.

Let's use the sashelp dataset 'cars' to explore the ins and outs of PROC FREQ. Example 6.1 shows simple syntax for executing PROC FREQ with one

Type	Frequency	Percent	Cumulative Frequency	Cumulative Percent
Hybrid	3	0.70	3	0.70
SUV	60	14.02	63	14.72
Sedan	262	61.21	325	75.93
Sports	49	11.45	374	87.38
Truck	24	5.61	398	92.99
Wagon	30	7.01	428	100.00

DriveTrain	Frequency	Percent	Cumulative Frequency	Cumulative Percent
All	92	21.50	92	21.50
Front	226	52.80	318	74.30
Rear	110	25.70	428	100.00

FIGURE 6.1. FREQUENCY Procedure Output.

variable. In cases where more than one variable is included in the TABLES statement (Example 6.2), the output includes separate frequency listings for each variable, like the ones in Figure 6.1.

EXAMPLE 6.1. FREQUENCY Procedure Syntax.

```
proc freq data = sashelp.cars;
tables type;
run;
```

EXAMPLE 6.2. FREQUENCY Procedure Syntax with Two Variables.

```
proc freq data = sashelp.cars;
tables type drivetrain;
run;
```

The output shown in Figure 6.1 provides information about the variable 'type.' The first column of information tells us that there are six distinct values for this variable: 'hybrid,' 'SUV,' and so on. The Frequency column tells us how many observations carry each variable value, while the Percent column indicates the percentage of observations that carry each variable value. For instance, when we look at the row of information for variable value 'SUV', we see that there are 60 observations with this value and that those observations make up 14.02% of our data. The last two columns provide cumulative information; there are 63 observations with variable values 'Hybrid' or 'SUV', which make up 14.72% of our data. This information is especially useful in instances where the categorical values are sequential in some way, such as levels of disease severity, income, and so forth.

As with most procedures, there are a handful of options that allow the user to manipulate the appearance of the output. For instance, the ORDER option allows the user to adjust the order in which the variable values appear in the table or list. By default, variables will appear in numerical or alphabetical order depending on their values. By setting the ORDER option equal to 'freq' as in Example 6.3, variable values will appear by descending frequency count. Figure 6.2 shows the exact same data as that in the first table of Figure 6.1, but the order in which the vehicle types are listed has been shuffled so that the type with the highest frequency appears first and is followed by the other values in descending order.

EXAMPLE 6.3. FREQUENCY Procedure Syntax with ORDER Option.

```
proc freq data = sashelp.cars order = freq;
tables type;
run;
```

Type	Frequency	Percent	Cumulative Frequency	Cumulative Percent
Sedan	262	61.21	262	61.21
SUV	60	14.02	322	75.23
Sports	49	11.45	371	86.68
Wagon	30	7.01	401	93.69
Truck	24	5.61	425	99.30
Hybrid	3	0.70	428	100.00

FIGURE 6.2. FREQUENCY Procedure Output with ORDER = FREQ Option.

Other ORDER options include FORMATTED, where values are printed in alphabetical order by the formatted value, and INTERNAL, where variables are printed in the order in which they appear in the dataset.

The PAGE option instructs SAS to print frequency tables/lists for each variable listed in the TABLES statement on a separate page. Syntax for employing the PAGE option is shown in Example 6.4.

EXAMPLE 6.4. FREQUENCY Procedure Syntax with PAGE Option.

```
proc freq data = sashelp.cars page;
tables type drivetrain;
run;
```

As a preliminary assessment of the relationship between two variables, the FREQUENCY procedure is also commonly used to calculate combined frequencies, often referred to as cross-tabular frequencies – in other words, categories created by combining the values of two or more variables. As shown in Example 6.5, placing an asterisk (*) between variables listed in the TABLES statement instructs SAS to calculate frequencies that are displayed in a table, such as the one in Figure 6.3.

EXAMPLE 6.5. FREQUENCY Procedure Syntax for Cross-Tabular Frequencies.

```
proc freq data = sashelp.cars;
tables type*drivetrain;
run;
```

Cross-tabular output provides cell count (frequency), overall percent, row percent, and column percent. The far-right column is similar to the information contained in Figure 6.2, and the bottom row of data provides comparable data for the variable 'drivetrain'. Again, let's look at the row of data for type equal to 'SUV'. The three columns labeled 'All', 'Front', and 'Rear' reflect the values for the variable 'drive train'. Among the 60 observations where type is equal to 'SUV', 38 have 'drivetrain' equal to 'all'. Those 38 observations make up 8.88% of all observations, 63.33% of the observations with 'type' equal to 'SUV' (row percent), and 41.30% of the observations with 'drivetrain' equal to 'all' (column percent).

Sometimes list-style output is preferable. When requesting list-style output for cross-tabular data, the TABLES statement must contain the LIST option as shown in Example 6.6; the resulting output is shown in Figure 6.4. The drawback to this output style is that it does not provide row and column percentages. However, as previously mentioned, it provides cumulative

Frequency Percent Row Pct Col Pct	Table of Type by DriveTrain			
		DriveTrain		
Type	All	Front	Rear	Total
Hybrid	0	3	0	3
	0.00	0.70	0.00	0.70
	0.00	100.00	0.00	
	0.00	1.33	0.00	
SUV	38	22	0	60
	8.88	5.14	0.00	14.02
	63.33	36.67	0.00	
	41.30	9.73	0.00	
Sedan	28	179	55	262
	6.54	41.82	12.85	61.21
	10.69	68.32	20.99	
	30.43	79.20	50.00	
Sports	5	8	36	49
	1.17	1.87	8.41	11.45
	10.20	16.33	73.47	
	5.43	3.54	32.73	
Truck	12	0	12	24
	2.80	0.00	2.80	5.61
	50.00	0.00	50.00	
	13.04	0.00	10.91	
Wagon	9	14	7	30
	2.10	3.27	1.64	7.01
	30.00	46.67	23.33	
	9.78	6.19	6.36	
Total	92	226	110	428
	21.50	52.80	25.70	100.00

FIGURE 6.3. Cross-Tabular Frequencies Produced by the FREQUENCY Procedure.

frequencies and percentages, which can be very useful when categories are sequential.

EXAMPLE 6.6. FREQUENCY Procedure Syntax for Cross-Tabular List-Style Frequencies.

```
proc freq data = sashelp.cars;
tables type*drivetrain/list;
run;
```

Type	DriveTrain	Frequency	Percent	Cumulative Frequency	Cumulative Percent
Hybrid	Front	3	0.70	3	0.70
SUV	All	38	8.88	41	9.58
SUV	Front	22	5.14	63	14.72
Sedan	All	28	6.54	91	21.26
Sedan	Front	179	41.82	270	63.08
Sedan	Rear	55	12.85	325	75.93
Sports	All	5	1.17	330	77.10
Sports	Front	8	1.87	338	78.97
Sports	Rear	36	8.41	374	87.38
Truck	All	12	2.80	386	90.19
Truck	Rear	12	2.80	398	92.99
Wagon	All	9	2.10	407	95.09
Wagon	Front	14	3.27	421	98.36
Wagon	Rear	7	1.64	428	100.00

FIGURE 6.4. List Style Cross-Tabular Frequencies Produced by the FREQUENCY Procedure.

THE MEANS PROCEDURE

PROC MEANS is most frequently used to describe the distribution of a continuous value. It can be used to calculate measures of central tendency and dispersion as well as to identify extreme values. Standard syntax (Example 6.7) and output (Figure 6.5) reveal the number of observations with data for each variable along with the mean, standard deviation, minimum, and maximum values for each variable.

EXAMPLE 6.7. MEANS Procedure Syntax.
```
proc means data = sashelp.cars;
run;
```

Syntax can be modified (Example 6.8) to include statistic keywords. When included in the PROC MEANS statement, these options specify which statistics to compute and in what order they should appear in the output (Figure 6.6). Table 6.1 contains a list of commonly used statistic keywords

Variable	Label	N	Mean	Std Dev	Minimum	Maximum
MSRP		428	32774.86	19431.72	10280.00	192465.00
Invoice		428	30014.70	17642.12	9875.00	173560.00
EngineSize	Engine Size (L)	428	3.1967290	1.1085947	1.3000000	8.3000000
Cylinders		426	5.8075117	1.5584426	3.0000000	12.0000000
Horsepower		428	215.8855140	71.8360316	73.0000000	500.0000000
MPG_City	MPG (City)	428	20.0607477	5.2382176	10.0000000	60.0000000
MPG_Highway	MPG (Highway)	428	26.8434579	5.7412007	12.0000000	66.0000000
Weight	Weight (LBS)	428	3577.95	758.9832146	1850.00	7190.00
Wheelbase	Wheelbase (IN)	428	108.1542056	8.3118130	89.0000000	144.0000000
Length	Length (IN)	428	186.3621495	14.3579913	143.0000000	238.0000000

FIGURE 6.5. MEANS Procedure Output.

that can be used in the MEANS procedure. A complete list can be found at the SAS support website (support.sas.com).

EXAMPLE 6.8. MEANS Procedure Syntax with MIN, MEDIAN, and MAX Keywords.

```
proc means data = sashelp.cars min median max;
run;
```

Variable	Label	Minimum	Median	Maximum
MSRP		10280.00	27635.00	192465.00
Invoice		9875.00	25294.50	173560.00
EngineSize	Engine Size (L)	1.3000000	3.0000000	8.3000000
Cylinders		3.0000000	6.0000000	12.0000000
Horsepower		73.0000000	210.0000000	500.0000000
MPG_City	MPG (City)	10.0000000	19.0000000	60.0000000
MPG_Highway	MPG (Highway)	12.0000000	26.0000000	66.0000000
Weight	Weight (LBS)	1850.00	3474.50	7190.00
Wheelbase	Wheelbase (IN)	89.0000000	107.0000000	144.0000000
Length	Length (IN)	143.0000000	187.0000000	238.0000000

FIGURE 6.6. MEANS Procedure Output with MIN, MEDIAN, and MAX Options.

Often we are only interested in the distribution of a single variable or a subset of variables. In Example 6.9 and Figure 6.7 we can see how the VAR statement provides an opportunity to specify which variables should be included in the MEANS procedure output. In this example, two variables are listed in the VAR statement and only those two variables appear in the resulting output.

EXAMPLE 6.9. **MEANS Procedure Syntax with VAR Statement.**

```
proc means data = sashelp.cars;
var msrp invoice;
run;
```

Variable	N	Mean	Std Dev	Minimum	Maximum
MSRP	428	32774.86	19431.72	10280.00	192465.00
Invoice	428	30014.70	17642.12	9875.00	173560.00

FIGURE 6.7. **MEANS Procedure Output with VAR Statement.**

TABLE 6.1. Selected Statistic Keywords for the MEANS Procedure.	
STATISTIC KEYWORD	PURPOSE
N, NMISS	Number of non-missing observations, number of observations
P1, P5, P25, P50, P75, P95, P99	Percentiles of the distribution
Q1, Q3	Quartiles of the distribution
MEAN, MEDIAN, MODE	Measures of central tendency
LCLM, UCLM	Lower and upper confidence limits for the mean

THE UNIVARIATE PROCEDURE

Standard PROC UNIVARIATE output provides similar information to the MEANS procedure, but is much more detailed by default. Also similar to PROC MEANS, the VAR statement is used to specify which variables will be included in the output. Simple syntax and default output are shown in Example 6.10 and Figures 6.8a and 6.8b, respectively.

EXAMPLE 6.10. **UNIVARIATE Procedure Syntax.**

```
proc univariate data = sashelp.cars;
var msrp;
run;
```

The UNIVARIATE Procedure
Variable: MSRP

Moments			
N	428	Sum Weights	428
Mean	32774.8551	Sum Observations	14027638
Std Deviation	19431.7167	Variance	377591613
Skewness	2.79809927	Kurtosis	13.8792055
Uncorrected SS	6.20985E11	Corrected SS	1.61232E11
Coeff Variation	59.2884899	Std Error Mean	939.267478

Basic Statistical Measures			
Location		Variability	
Mean	32774.86	Std Deviation	19432
Median	27635.00	Variance	377591613
Mode	13270.00	Range	182185
		Interquartile Range	18886

(a)

FIGURE 6.8A. UNIVARIATE Procedure Output.

In Figure 6.8a, the first two sections of PROC UNIVARIATE output specify 'moments' of the data such as the number of observations with non-missing values (N), skewness, and coefficient of variation. Basic statistical measures are included in the next table, along with corresponding measures of variability and the interquartile range. In Figure 6.8b, the next three sections of PROC UNIVARIATE output show tests for the location of the mean, including p-values, quantiles of the distribution, and extreme (lowest and highest) observations. In Chapter 8 we will discuss how PROC UNIVARIATE can also provide visual depictions of variable distributions using the plots option.

Tests for Location: Mu0=0				
Test	Statistic		p Value	
Student's t	t	34.89406	Pr > |t|	<.0001
Sign	M	214	Pr >= |M|	<.0001
Signed Rank	S	45903	Pr >= |S|	<.0001

Quantiles (Definition 5)	
Quantile	Estimate
100% Max	192465.0
99%	94820.0
95%	73195.0
90%	52795.0
75% Q3	39215.0
50% Median	27635.0
25% Q1	20329.5
10%	15460.0
5%	13670.0
1%	11155.0
0% Min	10280.0

Extreme Observations			
Lowest		Highest	
Value	Obs	Value	Obs
10280	207	94820	262
10539	169	121770	271
10760	383	126670	272
10995	346	128420	263
11155	208	192465	335

(b)

FIGURE 6.8B. UNIVARIATE Procedure Output.

THE CORR PROCEDURE

PROC CORR outputs a correlation matrix (Pearson Correlation Coefficients), which relays the relationship between two variables. As the coefficient moves closer to an absolute value of 1, the relationship becomes more perfect: in other words, a variable's correlation with itself is always 1. In Example 6.11 the syntax specifies three variables from the sashelp dataset cars.

The CORR Procedure

3 Variables: EngineSize Cylinders Horsepower

Simple Statistics							
Variable	N	Mean	Std Dev	Sum	Minimum	Maximum	Label
EngineSize	428	3.19673	1.10859	1368	1.30000	8.30000	Engine Size (L)
Cylinders	426	5.80751	1.55844	2474	3.00000	12.00000	
Horsepower	428	215.88551	71.83603	92399	73.00000	500.00000	

Pearson Correlation Coefficients Prob > |r| under H0: Rho=0 Number of Observations			
	EngineSize	Cylinders	Horsepower
EngineSize Engine Size (L)	1.00000	0.90800 <.0001	0.78743 <.0001
		428	426	428
Cylinders	0.90800 <.0001	1.00000	0.81034 <.0001
	426	426	426
Horsepower	0.78743 <.0001	0.81034 <.0001	1.00000
	428	426	428

FIGURE 6.9. CORR Procedure Output.

EXAMPLE **6.11. CORR Procedure Syntax.**

```
proc corr data = sashelp.cars;
var enginesize cylinders horsepower;
run;
```

Figure 6.9 shows the corresponding output from syntax in Example 6.11. Simple statistics for each variable are included (similar to PROC MEANS output), along with a table of correlation coefficients. Among the three variables, engine size and cylinders are the most highly correlated (r = 0.90800), and horsepower and engine size are the least correlated (0.78743), while the p-value for all possible correlations is significant (<0.0001).

Exploring the distribution of variables and assessing the relationship between those variables is a preliminary step in the analytic process. The four procedures outlined in this chapter provide a multifaceted toolkit for completing this task. In the next two chapters we will delve further into commonly used procedures and learn how they can help the programmer describe data to researchers.

TEST YOUR SKILLS

Use the sashelp dataset 'class' and the techniques described in Chapter 6 to accomplish the following tasks.

6.1 Create a frequency distribution for the variables 'sex' and 'age'.

6.2 Create a cross-tabular frequency distribution for the variables 'sex' and 'age'.

6.3 Identify the minimum, maximum, and mean values for the variable 'height'.

6.4 Identify the 20th, 40th, 60th, and 80th percentiles for the variable 'height'.

6.5 Identify the five lowest and five highest values for the variable 'height'.

6.6 Explore the correlation between the variables 'height', 'weight', and 'age'.

SOLUTIONS

6.1 Create a frequency distribution for the variables 'sex' and 'age'.

```
proc freq data = sashelp.class;
tables sex age;
run;
```

The FREQ Procedure

Sex	Frequency	Percent	Cumulative Frequency	Cumulative Percent
F	9	47.37	9	47.37
M	10	52.63	19	100.00

Age	Frequency	Percent	Cumulative Frequency	Cumulative Percent
11	2	10.53	2	10.53
12	5	26.32	7	36.84
13	3	15.79	10	52.63
14	4	21.05	14	73.68
15	4	21.05	18	94.74
16	1	5.26	19	100.00

6.2 Create a cross-tabular frequency distribution for the variables 'sex' and 'age'.

```
proc freq data = sashelp.class;
tables sex*age;
run;
```

The FREQ Procedure

Frequency Percent Row Pct Col Pct	Table of Sex by Age						
		Age					
Sex	11	12	13	14	15	16	Total
F	1	2	2	2	2	0	9
	5.26	10.53	10.53	10.53	10.53	0.00	47.37
	11.11	22.22	22.22	22.22	22.22	0.00	
	50.00	40.00	66.67	50.00	50.00	0.00	
M	1	3	1	2	2	1	10
	5.26	15.79	5.26	10.53	10.53	5.26	52.63
	10.00	30.00	10.00	20.00	20.00	10.00	
	50.00	60.00	33.33	50.00	50.00	100.00	
Total	2	5	3	4	4	1	19
	10.53	26.32	15.79	21.05	21.05	5.26	100.00

6.3 Identify the minimum, maximum, and mean values for the variable 'height'.

```
proc means data = sashelp.class min max mean;
var height;
run;
```

The MEANS Procedure

Analysis Variable : Height		
Minimum	Maximum	Mean
51.3000000	72.0000000	62.3368421

6.4 Identify the 20th, 40th, 60th, and 80th percentiles for the variable 'height'.

```
proc means data = sashelp.class p20 p40 p60 p80;
var height;
run;
```

The MEANS Procedure

Analysis Variable : Height			
20th Pctl	40th Pctl	60th Pctl	80th Pctl
57.3000000	62.5000000	64.3000000	66.5000000

6.5 Identify the five lowest and five highest values for the variable 'height'.

```
proc univariate data = sashelp.class;
var height;
run;
```

Extreme Observations			
Lowest		Highest	
Value	Obs	Value	Obs
51.3	11	66.5	14
56.3	13	66.5	19
56.5	2	67.0	17
57.3	6	69.0	1
57.5	18	72.0	15

6.6 Explore the correlation between the variables 'height', 'weight', and 'age'.

```
proc corr data = sashelp.class;
var height weight age;
run;
```

The CORR Procedure

3 **Variables:** Height Weight Age

Simple Statistics						
Variable	N	Mean	Std Dev	Sum	Minimum	Maximum
Height	19	62.33684	5.12708	1184	51.30000	72.00000
Weight	19	100.02632	22.77393	1901	50.50000	150.00000
Age	19	13.31579	1.49267	253.00000	11.00000	16.00000

Pearson Correlation Coefficients, N = 19 Prob > |r| under H0: Rho=0			
	Height	Weight	Age
Height	1.00000	0.87779	0.81143
		<.0001	<.0001
Weight	0.87779	1.00000	0.74089
	<.0001		0.0003
Age	0.81143	0.74089	1.00000
	<.0001	0.0003	

CHAPTER 7

More about Common Procedures

In this chapter, we delve deeper into the simple statistics procedures introduced in Chapter 6 and discuss how these procedures can be employed to accomplish even more tasks. Using BY and CLASS statements, output can be stratified by groups of interest. Various options for reporting missing values (MISSPRINT, MISSING, NMISS) are appropriate and useful depending on the purpose of the output. Simple statistical tests can be performed and results featured in the output while new datasets can be created containing the information provided by this output.

STRATIFIED OUTPUT USING THE BY AND CLASS STATEMENTS

Frequently, data needs to be reviewed in a stratified format. Variables like height and weight typically need to be reviewed separately for males and females, and in a clinical trial, patient outcomes must often be reviewed separately for each treatment group. Using a BY or CLASS statement allows the programmer to access the full functionality of a procedure in a stratified setting. A BY statement can be used in the MEANS, FREQ, UNIVARIATE, and CORR procedures. Before a BY statement can be invoked, the dataset must first be sorted according to the variable to be specified in that statement.

The MEANS Procedure

Origin=Asia

	Analysis Variable : MSRP			
N	**Mean**	**Std Dev**	**Minimum**	**Maximum**
158	24741.32	11321.07	10280.00	89765.00

Origin=Europe

	Analysis Variable : MSRP			
N	**Mean**	**Std Dev**	**Minimum**	**Maximum**
123	48349.80	25318.60	16999.00	192465.00

Origin=USA

	Analysis Variable : MSRP			
N	**Mean**	**Std Dev**	**Minimum**	**Maximum**
147	28377.44	11711.98	10995.00	81795.00

FIGURE **7.1. MEANS Procedure Output with BY Statement.**

The CLASS statement can only be used in the MEANS and UNIVARIATE procedure and does not require that the dataset be presorted.

Let's continue with the sashelp dataset 'cars.' Suppose we are curious about any differences in the distribution of 'msrp' based on 'origin.' Since we will be using a BY statement, we must first sort the dataset according to the variable we will use in that statement. SAS does not allow us to sort a dataset in the permanent sashelp library, so first we will create a work dataset and then sort it. Finally, we use the MEANS procedure with a BY statement (Example 7.1).

EXAMPLE **7.1. MEANS Procedure Syntax with BY Statement.**

```
data cars; set sashelp.cars; run;
proc sort data = cars; by origin; run;
proc means data = cars;
var msrp ;
by origin;
run;
```

Figure 7.1 shows the resulting output. It is exactly like the output that would result from executing a PROC MEANS without a BY statement, but the output is stratified by the variable 'origin.' A quick review of this output tells the programmer that the distributions for Asia and the United States are relatively similar, while the distribution for Europe sits in a higher range and has a larger standard deviation and fewer contributing observations (N).

Invoking a BY statement in the FREQUENCY, UNIVARIATE, and CORR procedure has a similar effect. While the cars dataset is sorted by 'origin', try the syntax in Examples 7.2, 7.3, and 7.4. The resulting output takes the same form as it would without a BY statement, but the information is stratified by 'origin', allowing for a visual comparison of the distributions based on that variable.

EXAMPLE 7.2. FREQUENCY Procedure Syntax with BY Statement.

```
proc freq data = cars;
tables type*drivetrain/ list;
by origin;
run;
```

EXAMPLE 7.3. UNIVARIATE Procedure Syntax with BY Statement.

```
proc univariate data = cars;
var msrp;
by origin;
run;
```

EXAMPLE 7.4. CORR Procedure Syntax with BY Statement.

```
proc corr data = cars;
var msrp invoice;
by origin;
run;
```

Using a CLASS statement reaps similar output to that resulting from a BY statement, with the added benefit that data does not need to be sorted before the statement is executed. However, CLASS statements cannot be used with the FREQUENCY or CORR procedures. In the syntax shown in Example 7.5 the CLASS statement is used in the MEANS procedure, with resulting output shown in Figure 7.2. In this example we specify two variables in the VAR statement, and the resulting output is stratified by 'origin', which is specified in the CLASS statement. Rather than having three separate tables (as in Figure 7.1), the descriptive statistics for 'MSRP' and 'Invoice' are displayed in a single table, stratified by 'Origin'. The CLASS variable is listed in the far-left column and the Variable column describes which variable each row of data represents.

The MEANS Procedure

Origin	N Obs	Variable	N	Mean	Std Dev	Minimum	Maximum
Asia	158	MSRP	158	24741.32	11321.07	10280.00	89765.00
		Invoice	158	22602.18	9842.98	9875.00	79978.00
Europe	123	MSRP	123	48349.80	25318.60	16999.00	192465.00
		Invoice	123	44395.08	23080.37	15437.00	173560.00
USA	147	MSRP	147	28377.44	11711.98	10995.00	81795.00
		Invoice	147	25949.34	10518.72	10319.00	74451.00

FIGURE **7.2. MEANS Procedure Output with CLASS Statement.**

EXAMPLE **7.5. MEANS Procedure Syntax with CLASS Statement.**

```
proc means data = sashelp.cars;
var msrp invoice;
class origin;
run;
```

Example 7.6 provides syntax for employing the CLASS statement in the UNIVARIATE procedure. Submitting this syntax will result in output that is nearly identical to that produced by the syntax in Example 7.3.

EXAMPLE **7.6. UNIVARIATE Procedure Syntax with CLASS Statement.**

```
proc univariate data = sashelp.cars;
var msrp;
class origin;
run;
```

MISSING DATA

Another important piece of preliminary data exploration is the identification and handling of missing values. The FREQUENCY and MEANS procedures offer some useful options for identifying missing values and determining their location. Example 7.7 shows standard syntax for the FREQUENCY procedure as discussed in Chapter 6. Example 7.8 includes the MISSPRINT option. This

The FREQ Procedure

Frequency Percent Row Pct Col Pct	Table of Cylinders by DriveTrain			
		DriveTrain		
Cylinders	All	Front	Rear	Total
.	0	0	2	.
	.	.	.	.
	.	.	.	.
	.	.	.	.
3	0	1	0	1
	0.00	0.23	0.00	0.23
	0.00	100.00	0.00	
	0.00	0.44	0.00	
4	18	107	11	136
	4.23	25.12	2.58	31.92
	13.24	78.68	8.09	
	19.57	47.35	10.19	
5	4	3	0	7
	0.94	0.70	0.00	1.64
	57.14	42.86	0.00	
	4.35	1.33	0.00	

FIGURE 7.3. FREQ Procedure Output with MISSPRINT Option.

option specifies that missings appear as a variable value and therefore have their own row/column in the cross-tabular output.

EXAMPLE 7.7. FREQ Procedure Syntax.
```
proc freq data = sashelp.cars;
tables cylinders*drivetrain;
run;
```

EXAMPLE 7.8. FREQ Procedure Syntax with MISSPRINT Option.
```
proc freq data = sashelp.cars;
tables cylinders*drivetrain/ missprint;
run;
```

In Figure 7.3 we can see that there are two observations in the 'cars' dataset with a missing value for the variable 'cylinders', both of which have 'drivetrain' equal to 'rear'. Notably, these observations are not included in any of the percentages in the table.

The FREQ Procedure

Cylinders	DriveTrain	Frequency	Percent	Cumulative Frequency	Cumulative Percent
.	Rear	2	0.47	2	0.47
3	Front	1	0.23	3	0.70
4	All	18	4.21	21	4.91
4	Front	107	25.00	128	29.91
4	Rear	11	2.57	139	32.48
5	All	4	0.93	143	33.41
5	Front	3	0.70	146	34.11
6	All	41	9.58	187	43.69
6	Front	98	22.90	285	66.59
6	Rear	51	11.92	336	78.50
8	All	28	6.54	364	85.05
8	Front	16	3.74	380	88.79
8	Rear	43	10.05	423	98.83
10	All	1	0.23	424	99.07
10	Rear	1	0.23	425	99.30
12	Front	1	0.23	426	99.53
12	Rear	2	0.47	428	100.00

FIGURE 7.4. FREQ Procedure Output with MISSING Option.

In Example 7.9 the programmer is requesting list-style frequencies using the LIST option. The MISSPRINT option cannot be used with the LIST option, but the MISSING option is a good alternative. As shown Figure 7.4, this combination of options provides a frequency listing where missing values are included in the cumulative frequency and percentages.

EXAMPLE 7.9. FREQ Procedure Syntax with MISSING Option.

```
proc freq data = sashelp.cars;
tables cylinders*drivetrain/list missing;
run;
```

Generally speaking, using the FREQUENCY procedure to examine missing values allows the user not only to identify where the missing values are but also to characterize those observations with respect to the other variables in the dataset. This kind of information is important when evaluating bias in the data. If the goal is more simple, e.g. straightforward counts of missing values by variable, the MEANS procedure produces sufficient detail using the N and NMISS options. However, this approach will only produce information about numeric variables (i.e., character variables will be excluded). Syntax displayed in Example 7.10 results in output shown in Figure 7.5. This output provides a list of all numeric variables in the dataset (because we did not include a VAR statement) with columns that specify the number of non-missing (n) and missing (nmiss) values for each variable.

EXAMPLE 7.10. MEANS Procedure Syntax with N and NMISS Options.

```
proc means data = sashelp.cars n nmiss mean std;
run;
```

The MEANS Procedure

Variable	Label	N	N Miss	Mean	Std Dev
MSRP		428	0	32774.86	19431.72
Invoice		428	0	30014.70	17642.12
EngineSize	Engine Size (L)	428	0	3.1967290	1.1085947
Cylinders		426	2	5.8075117	1.5584426
Horsepower		428	0	215.8855140	71.8360316
MPG_City	MPG (City)	428	0	20.0607477	5.2382176
MPG_Highway	MPG (Highway)	428	0	26.8434579	5.7412007
Weight	Weight (LBS)	428	0	3577.95	758.9832146
Wheelbase	Wheelbase (IN)	428	0	108.1542056	8.3118130
Length	Length (IN)	428	0	186.3621495	14.3579913

FIGURE 7.5. MEANS Procedure Output with N and NMISS Options.

OUTPUT DATASETS

Using procedures to create new datasets is another useful trick for programmers. In these datasets, commonly referred to as *output datasets*, variable values, frequency counts, percentages, and test statistics are actually variables. Typically the NOPRINT option, which suppresses procedure output in both the Output Window and the Results Viewer, is included in the PROC statement when an output dataset is the goal (Examples 7.11 and 7.12).

	Cylinders	DriveTrain	Frequency Count	Percent of Total Frequency
1	.	Rear	2	.
2	3	Front	1	0.234741784
3	4	All	18	4.2253521127
4	4	Front	107	25.117370892
5	4	Rear	11	2.5821596244
6	5	All	4	0.9389671362
7	5	Front	3	0.7042253521
8	6	All	41	9.6244131455
9	6	Front	98	23.004694836
10	6	Rear	51	11.971830986
11	8	All	28	6.5727699531
12	8	Front	16	3.7558685446
13	8	Rear	43	10.093896714
14	10	All	1	0.234741784
15	10	Rear	1	0.234741784
16	12	Front	1	0.234741784
17	12	Rear	2	0.4694835681

FIGURE 7.6. FREQ Procedure Output Dataset 'freqcount' from Example 7.11.'

When creating a new dataset from the FREQ procedure, as shown in Example 7.11, syntax includes the 'OUT =' option where the output dataset is named. In the resulting dataset (Figure 7.6) each observation (row) represents one of the cells in a standard cross-tabular output. Each variable (column) reflects either a variable or option specified in the TABLES statement. For instance, in Figure 7.6, the columns 'Cylinders' and 'DriveTrain' are variables from the 'cars' dataset and the columns 'Frequency Count' and 'Percent of Total Frequency' are data points from default FREQ procedure output.

EXAMPLE 7.11. FREQ Procedure Syntax for Output Dataset Using 'OUT = ' in the TABLES Statement.

```
proc freq data = sashelp.cars noprint;
tables cylinders*drivetrain/ out = freqcount;
run;
```

	DriveTrain	_TYPE_	_FREQ_	AverageMSRP
1		0	428	$32,775
2	All	1	92	$36,483
3	Front	1	226	$24,783
4	Rear	1	110	$46,094

FIGURE 7.7. MEANS Procedure Output Dataset 'summary_stat' from Example 7.12.

Output datasets can also be produced by the MEANS procedure, using slightly different syntax (Example 7.12). The statistic of interest, in this case MEAN, is specified in the PROC MEANS statement along with the NOPRINT option and details about the output dataset are specified in the OUTPUT statement. The output dataset is named in the 'OUT = ' option and the variable for the mean is specified in the MEAN = option. Figure 7.7 displays the number of contributing observations (_FREQ_) and mean value (AverageMSRP) for each level of the variable specified in the CLASS statement. The levels of the class variable are listed in the column 'DriveTrain'; _TYPE_ is used to summarize the values that represent the subgroups of the class variable. The value of _TYPE_ changes based on the combination of variables included the class statement (or lack thereof).

EXAMPLE 7.12. **MEANS Procedure Syntax for Output Dataset.**

```
proc means data = sashelp.cars mean noprint;
var msrp;
class drivetrain;
output out = summary_stat mean = AverageMSRP;
run;
```

STATISTICAL TESTS

While the goal of this text is not to teach statistical testing techniques using SAS software, it is worth a quick mention of the types of statistical testing that can be performed as part of the procedures discussed thus far. While many complex statistical analyses require more advanced procedures in SAS, some basic tests of association can be performed within simpler procedures. It is not uncommon for researchers and investigators to use these simpler testing methods during the final stages of data cleaning and early phases of data analysis.

Statistics for Table of Cylinders by DriveTrain

Statistic	DF	Value	Prob
Chi-Square	12	93.6394	<.0001
Likelihood Ratio Chi-Square	12	101.4141	<.0001
Mantel-Haenszel Chi-Square	1	8.2163	0.0042
Phi Coefficient		0.4688	
Contingency Coefficient		0.4245	
Cramer's V		0.3315	

WARNING: 57% of the cells have expected counts less than 5. Chi-Square may not be a valid test.

Effective Sample Size = 426
Frequency Missing = 2

Summary Statistics for Cylinders by DriveTrain

Cochran-Mantel-Haenszel Statistics (Based on Table Scores)				
Statistic	Alternative Hypothesis	DF	Value	Prob
1	Nonzero Correlation	1	8.2163	0.0042
2	Row Mean Scores Differ	6	13.8348	0.0315
3	General Association	12	93.4196	<.0001

Effective Sample Size = 426
Frequency Missing = 2

FIGURE 7.8. FREQ Procedure Output with CHISQ and CMH Options.

In its standard form, the CORR procedure is a basic statistical test of association. Employing the T option in the PROC MEANS statement provides student's t-test statistics. The FREQUENCY procedure offers several options for test statistics of association. Example 7.13 shows syntax including the options for chi-square (CHISQ) and Cochran Mantel-Hantzel (CMH) test statistics within the FREQUENCY procedure. Corresponding output (Figure 7.8) includes standard cross-tabular output along with two additional tables. The information in these tables can be used to

describe the association between the variables specified in the TABLES
statement.

EXAMPLE 7.13.   FREQ Procedure Syntax with CHISQ and CMH Options.
```
proc freq data = sashelp.cars;
tables cylinders*drivetrain /chisq cmh;
run;
```

TEST YOUR SKILLS

Exercises in the portions use the dataset sashelp.shoes.

7.1 Determine if there are any missing observations in the data.
    (Hint: for numeric variables use Proc Means and for character variables
    use Proc Freq)
7.2 Investigate the different subsidiaries in the United States.
7.3 What product produces the highest sales in New York?
7.4 Which region has the highest correlation between number of stores and
    total sales?

SOLUTIONS

7.1 Determine if there are any missing observations in the data.

```
proc contents data = sashelp.shoes order = varnum; run;

proc means data = sashelp.shoes nmiss mean;
var stores--returns; run;

proc freq data = sashelp.shoes;
tables region--subsidiary/list missing; run;
```

7.2 Investigate the different subsidiaries in the United States.

```
Proc freq data = sashelp.shoes;
where region = 'United States';
tables Region*Subsidiary/list;
run;
```

Region	Subsidiary	Frequency	Percent	Cumulative Frequency	Cumulative Percent
United States	Chicago	8	20.00	8	20.00
United States	Los Angeles	8	20.00	16	40.00
United States	Minneapolis	8	20.00	24	60.00
United States	New York	8	20.00	32	80.00
United States	Seattle	8	20.00	40	100.00

7.3   What product produces the highest sales in New York?

```
Proc means data = sashelp.shoes max ;
var sales;
class product;
where subsidiary= 'New York';
run;
```

Analysis Variable : Sales Total Sales		
Product	N Obs	Maximum
Boot	1	97151.00
Men's Casual	1	456985.00
Men's Dress	1	191755.00
Sandal	1	554.0000000
Slipper	1	252758.00
Sport Shoe	1	22190.00
Women's Casual	1	178842.00
Women's Dress	1	288972.00

7.4   Which region has the highest correlation between number of stores and total sales?

```
Proc corr data = sashelp.shoes;
by region;
var stores sales;
run;
```

The CORR Procedure

Region=Asia

2 Variables: Stores Sales

Simple Statistics

Variable	N	Mean	Std Dev	Sum	Minimum	Maximum	Label
Stores	14	4.64286	6.48794	65.00000	1.00000	21.00000	Number of Stores
Sales	14	32874	48880	460231	937.00000	149013	Total Sales

Pearson Correlation Coefficients, N = 14
Prob > |r| under H0: Rho=0

	Stores	Sales
Stores Number of Stores	1.00000	0.84239 0.0002
Sales Total Sales	0.84239 0.0002	1.00000

CHAPTER 8

Data Visualization

A SAS programmer is rarely limited to displaying data in only one way; various paths can be taken to produce similar tables and plots. Determining which procedure and graphical output are best for the task is a decision specific to the user and the needs of the project. When sharing results with a group, it may be necessary to include more than one representation in order to help everyone understand the data. The purpose of this chapter is to (1) illustrate a sampling of methods for creating output that is visually diverse yet conveys identical information, and (2) to describe how the Output Delivery System (ODS) can be used to maximize the utility of SAS data visualization tools by exporting SAS output to other software. In Chapter 6 we discussed creating tables and list-style output for both data management and processing purposes. In this chapter we take these tasks one step further using some of the same procedures in combination with ODS statistical graphics to create graphical style output. We will also discuss additional SAS procedures such as GCHART and GPLOT, which are designed specifically for plotting data.

USING THE OUTPUT DELIVERY SYSTEM (ODS)

In this chapter we will introduce the output delivery system (ODS) and the two ways we use this indispensable SAS feature. First, ODS statements can be used to export SAS output to specific destinations. The programmer can choose how and where SAS output is stored as well as has control over its format. Second, ODS Statistical Graphics can be used to create visually appealing and printer-friendly graphics.

Example 8.1 shows the necessary syntax to direct output to a specific RTF destination. The statement to specify destination must include a file type and path. Literal syntax can be thought of a as a sandwich; it opens at the top of the procedure and closes at the bottom. The ODS RTF CLOSE statement closes the RTF destination; if there were subsequent syntax run requesting output, it would not be sent to the destination. Other examples of destinations where graphics can be displayed are HTML, PDF, and CSV.

EXAMPLE 8.1. Basic ODS Syntax.
```
Ods rtf file='C:\stats.rtf';

Proc print data=sashelp.class;
Run;

Ods rtf close;
```

To ensure results are created in HTML format (output to the results viewer), go to tools > options > preferences > under the results tab and make sure the "create HTML" box is checked. Viewing in HTML is especially important when using the ODS graphics statement to create a plot, explained in Example 8.3.

CREATING PLOTS FROM PROCS

The FREQUENCY Procedure

The FREQUENCY procedure produces tables and listings. Output can be requested for one variable or for a combination of variables. Procedure options (i.e., TREND, MEASURES, CL) and additional statements (i.e., PLOTS) are used to create detailed output and graphics. In Example 8.2 we use PROC FREQ to learn about the variable type in the sashelp dataset 'cars.' Output in Figure 8.1 indicates that car type 'Sedan' reflects 61% (N = 262) of the observations in this dataset.

The SAS System

The FREQ Procedure

Type	Frequency	Percent	Cumulative Frequency	Cumulative Percent
Hybrid	3	0.70	3	0.70
SUV	60	14.02	63	14.72
Sedan	262	61.21	325	75.93
Sports	49	11.45	374	87.38
Truck	24	5.61	398	92.99
Wagon	30	7.01	428	100.00

FIGURE 8.1. Standard FREQUENCY Procedure Output.

EXAMPLE 8.2. Syntax for the FREQUENCY Procedure.

```
proc freq data=sashelp.cars;
tables type/list; run;
```

In Example 8.3 we look more closely at the car type 'Sedan' and its distribution of number of cylinders by creating a plot. The PLOTS option specifies the type (two-way stacked) of frequency plot to produce. If no type is specified, SAS will produce a bar chart as the default. In order to have results that include a bar chart, ODS graphics must be enabled. Using 'ODS graphics on' and 'ods graphics off' at the beginning and end of the submitted syntax requests the plots be shown in the results viewer. If these commands are not used, a warning message appears in the log: "WARNING: You must enable ODS graphics before requesting plots."

EXAMPLE 8.3. FREQUENCY Procedure Syntax for Creating and Exporting a Plot.

```
ods graphics on;
proc freq data=sashelp.cars;
where type = 'Sedan';
tables type*cylinders/
plots=freqplot(twoway=stacked);
title 'Type of Car by Number of Cylinders';
run;
ods graphics off;
```

Type of Car by Number of Cylinders

The FREQ Procedure

Frequency Percent Row Pct Col Pct	Table of Type by Cylinders					
		Cylinders				
Type	4	5	6	8	12	Total
Sedan	96 36.64 36.64 100.00	6 2.29 2.29 100.00	120 45.80 45.80 100.00	38 14.50 14.50 100.00	2 0.76 0.76 100.00	262 100.00
Total	96 36.64	6 2.29	120 45.80	38 14.50	2 0.76	262 100.00

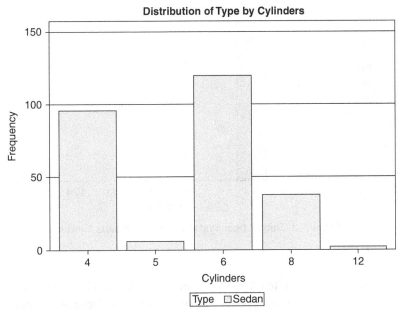

Distribution of Type by Cylinders

FIGURE 8.2. FREQUENCY Procedure Output from Syntax in Example 8.3.

The GCHART Procedure

Another way to accomplish the same task, without using ODS, is to utilize the GCHART procedure. PROC GCHART is a tool specifically for plotting data. Inclusion of different statements alters the graphic output. For example, the VBAR statement creates a vertical bar chart and the HBAR statement creates

Type of Car by Number of Cylinders

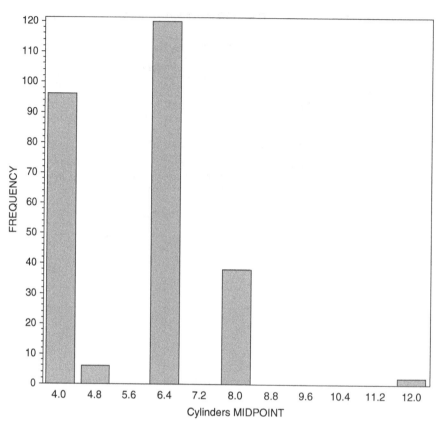

FIGURE 8.3. Output from Syntax 8.4 in the Results Viewer.

a horizontal bar chart. The GCHART procedure can also be used to make pie charts. As always, there are plenty of options that can be used to customize the output, which in this case are graphics. More extensive documentation of these options is available at the SAS Support website, http://support.sas .com.

Example 8.4 requests a vertical bar chart of frequency of cylinders for the car type 'Sedan'. Figure 8.3, output from the results viewer, reflects the same information as the chart in Figure 8.2, but is visually just a bit different.

EXAMPLE 8.4. **Syntax for the GCHART Procedure.**

```
proc gchart data = sashelp.cars;
where type = 'Sedan';
vbar cylinders;
run;
```

The UNIVARIATE Procedure

PROC UNIVARIATE provides information about the distribution of a variable; the plots option can be used to create a visual description of this distribution. First, with ODS graphics off, we will look at the histogram and box plot for the variable 'mpg_city' in the sashelp, cars dataset 'Cars' (Example 8.5). With or without the PLOTS option, descriptive information is output (Figure 8.4). Notice the quantiles in Figure 8.4; this information is what we want to convey in the plot.

EXAMPLE 8.5. **UNIVARIATE Procedure Syntax for Creating a Plot; ODS Graphics OFF.**

```
proc univariate data = sashelp.cars plots;
var mpg_city;
run;
```

Quantiles (Definition 5)	
Level	Quantile
100% Max	60.0
99%	36.0
95%	29.0
90%	26.0
75% Q3	21.5
50% Median	19.0
25% Q1	17.0
10%	15.0
5%	14.0
1%	12.0
0% Min	10.0

FIGURE 8.4. **UNIVARIATE Output for Variable MPG_City.**

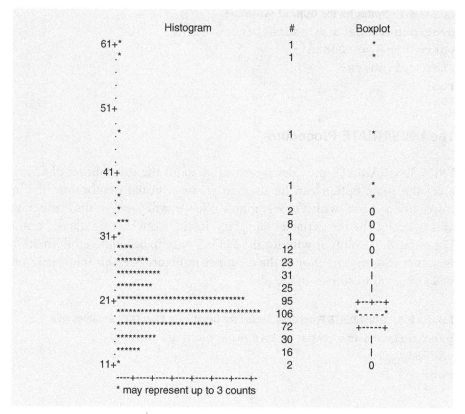

FIGURE 8.5. Univariate Output variable MPG_City; ODS Graphics OFF.

Results Viewer output with ODS turned off is shown in Figure 8.5. The histogram indicates the overall distribution; the numbers on the right (#) are indicative of the number of observations having values that fall within the range on the left column. A boxplot tells us about the quartile distribution of the data. The boxes represent the lower and upper quartiles while the line through the middle indicates the median.

Submitting the same syntax with ODS Graphics turned on (see Example 8.3 for ODS syntax) will result in the output displayed in Figure 8.6. The output in Figure 8.6 is much more visually appealing and is often the preferred method for reporting data. In either format (ODS on or off) these graphics quickly provide easily interpreted summary information, which allows for simple comparisons of data.

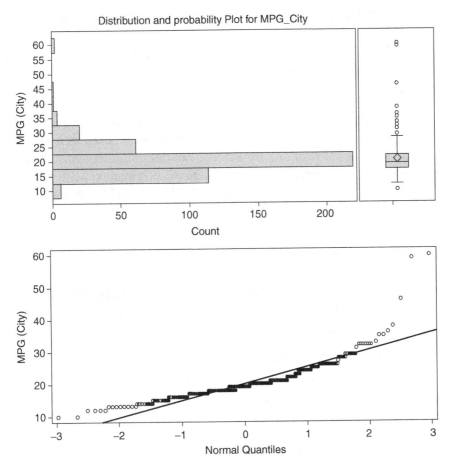

FIGURE 8.6. UNIVARIATE Output for Variable MPG_City; ODS Graphics ON.

The CORR Procedure

Standard output from PROC CORR displays simple statistics and Pearson correlation coefficients in the form of a correlation matrix (Chapter 6). Within PROC CORR, a scatterplot matrix can also be requested by including the PLOTS option and turning ODS graphics on as shown in Example 8.6. By default SAS only allows 5,000 points and the sashelp dataset 'cars' requires processing of more than that. In order to override the default we have included the MAXPOINTS = NONE option.

EXAMPLE 8.6. Syntax for Requesting Scatterplot Matrix in the CORR Procedure.

```
ods graphics on;
proc corr data=sashelp.cars nomiss plots(MAXPOINTS=NONE)=matrix;
var enginesize --weight; run;
ods graphics off;
```

Graphics are an extremely helpful way to understand the relationship between selected variables. Scatterplot matrices can be used as a graphical representation of correlations for several variables simultaneously and are easily output by simple additions to PROC CORR syntax. MPG_Highway and MPG_City are highly correlated (.9410). Weight and horsepower have a lower correlation (.6308).

The GPLOT Procedure

Another way to explore these differences graphically is to use PROC GPLOT. We will utilize ODS in this example to output our plot to Microsoft Word as a rich text file (Example 8.7).

EXAMPLE 8.7. Syntax for PROC GPLOT.

```
ods rtf file = 'C:\foldername\gplot.rtf';

proc gplot data =sashelp.cars;
plot mpg_highway*mpg_city weight*horsepower;
run;
quit;

ods rtf close;
```

Figure 8.7 and Figure 8.8 are visually very similar for the selected combination of variables. A higher correlation is depicted by values that create a straigher line (sloped upward). Notice the differences in the "lines" created in Figure 8.8 on the left representing .9410 and on the right .6308. The plot representing the higher correlation shows a visually tighter line and the plot for the lower correlation is more spread out.

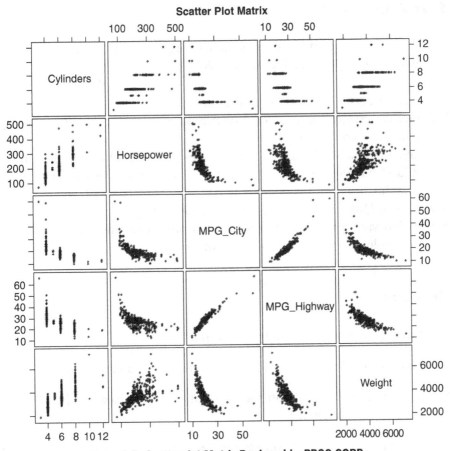

FIGURE 8.7. Scatterplot Matrix Produced by PROC CORR.

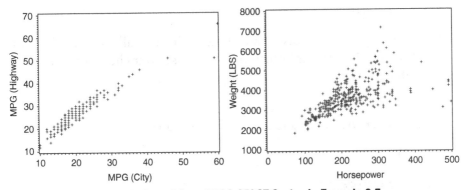

FIGURE 8.8. Output from PROC GPLOT Syntax in Example 8.7.

TEST YOUR SKILLS

Use the sashelp dataset 'Class' and the techniques described in this chapter in order to accomplish the following tasks.

8.1 Investigate the distribution of the variable 'Age'.
8.2 Save the created output on age distributions as an excel file (.csv) to the location of your choice.
8.3 Create a new work dataset named 'Ages', include all variables from the "Class" file. Plot this information by sex. Use your choice of method for graphing.
8.4 What is Quantile 1 and 3 for the variable height?
8.5 Which variable could be used to help predict another variable? Use a scatterplot to visually display this correlation.

SOLUTIONS

8.1 Investigate the distribution of the variable 'Age'.

```
proc freq data = sashelp.class; tables age; run;
```

8.2 Save the created output on age distributions as an excel file (.csv) to the location of your choice.

```
ods csv file = "C:\freq.csv";
proc freq data = sashelp.class; tables age; run;
ods csv close;
```

8.3 Create a new work dataset named 'Ages', include all variables from the "Class" file. Plot this information by sex. Use your choice of method for graphing.

```
data ages; set sashelp.class; run;
proc sort data = ages ; by sex; run;
```

Proc Freq:

```
ods graphics on;
proc freq data=ages;
by sex;
```

Age distribution by Sex

The FREQ Procedure

Sex=F

Age	Frequency	Percent	Cumulative Frequency	Cumulative Percent
11	1	11.11	1	11.11
12	2	22.22	3	33.33
13	2	22.22	5	55.56
14	2	22.22	7	77.78
15	2	22.22	9	100.00

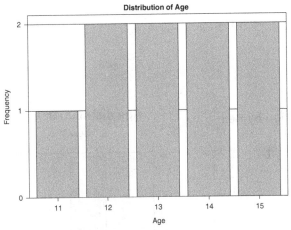

Distribution of Age

Age distribution by Sex

The FREQ Procedure

Sex=M

Age	Frequency	Percent	Cumulative Frequency	Cumulative Percent
11	1	10.00	1	10.00
12	3	30.00	4	40.00
13	1	10.00	5	50.00
14	2	20.00	7	70.00
15	2	20.00	9	90.00
16	1	10.00	10	100.00

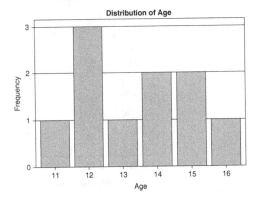

Distribution of Age

```
tables age/
plots=freqplot(twoway = stacked);
title 'Age distribution by Sex';
run;
ods graphics off;
```

Proc GChart:

```
proc gchart data = ages;
by sex;
vbar age;
run;
```

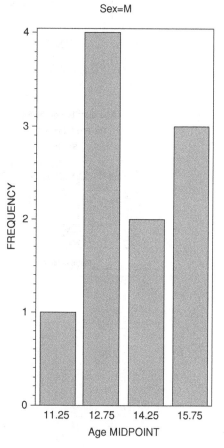

8.4 What is Quantile 1 and 3 for the variable height?

```
proc univariate data = ages; var height; run;
```

$$Q1 = 57.5, Q3 = 66.5$$

8.5 Which variable could be used to help predict another variable? Use a scatterplot to visually display this correlation.

```
proc corr data = ages; run;

proc gplot data =ages;
plot height*weight;
run;
quit;
```

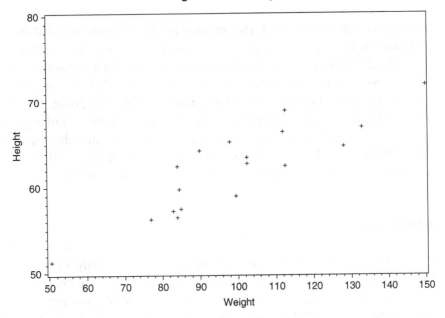

Age distribution by Sex

CHAPTER 9

JMP as an Alternative

In any data-reporting project, the finished product is only useful if the programmer has taken time to familiarize themselves with the data and determine the optimal way to represent it. JMP software from SAS is a visual and interactive tool with a focus on "statistical discovery." Using JMP, the programmer can easily explore the data, allowing curiosity to be their guide. JMP has a family of products that include Pro, Clinical, and Genomics. Detailed product information can be found at www.jmp.com/software. In this chapter we will use JMP Pro 10 with a tight focus on the most useful pieces of this product in relation to data management and using JMP in combination with SAS.

ABOUT JMP

JMP can be a great alternative for non-SAS users to easily view, explore, understand, and summarize data. This visual and interactive product allows anyone to explore data without the burden of heavy-duty programming. JMP incorporates both statistical and graphical techniques; it offers point, click, and drag capabilities, and since it is built for discovery, options allow the user to create graphs, refine their properties, or simply begin again with a just few mouse clicks. This product can also be used as a compliment to larger statistical analysis packages for ease of data importing as well as for the visually dynamic ways JMP can help the user truly get inside their data.

ACCESSING DATA

JMP, like SAS, offers sample data that can be accessed through the help menu. However, we would like to use a file from SAS that we have already created. Let's take a look at the datafile 'Ages', previously created in the Test your Skills section of Chapter 8. Using the syntax in Example 9.1, produce the dataset 'ages' and save it to the location of your choice.

EXAMPLE 9.1 Create SAS Dataset to Open in JMP

```
libname x 'Desktop';
data x.ages; set sashelp.class;
run;
```

FIGURE 9.1. SAS Dataset as an Open JMP Data Table in JMP Pro.

Next we are going to locate the ages.sas7bdat file and open it in JMP. To do this, open JMP and in the top left corner click File > Open. Then change "Files of Type" to "All Files", select your file, and click open. The dataset should now be visible in the JMP window (Figure 9.1). On the far left there are three boxes: the first one shows the name of the dataset; the second one labeled 'Columns' shows the number, names, and types of variables; and the third one labeled 'Rows' describes the observations in the open dataset.

EXPLORING VARIABLES AND DISTRIBUTIONS

From within a JMP data table, information about variables can easily be viewed and edited. Similar to selecting "column attributes" in SAS (Figure 2.2), double-clicking the variable name (the first cell) in JMP opens the box shown in Figure 9.2. In this window the programmer can change

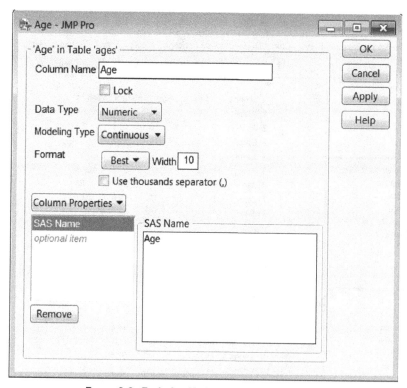

FIGURE 9.2. Exploring Variable Attributes in JMP.

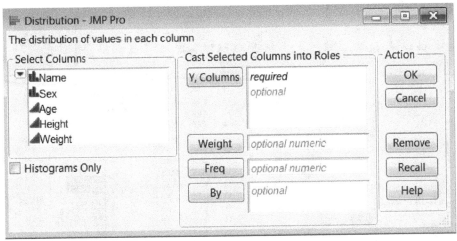

FIGURE 9.3. DISTRIBUTION Window in JMP.

names, data type, modeling type, format, and column properties. Selecting the APPLY button finalizes these changes. If no changes need to be made, selecting OK will simply close the window.

The analyze menu (on the toolbar) offers options for producing statistics and performing data analysis. On the toolbar, selecting Analyze > Distribution opens the window shown in Figure 9.3. Select, drag, and drop the variable of interest to the "Y, Columns" box and then click OK. On the far-right side of the JMP window, output is produced that is similar to the UNIVARIATE Procedure in SAS (Figures 8.4 and 8.6). Information about the variable's distribution is depicted by a list of quantiles along with a histogram (Figure 9.4).

A lot of JMP output is interactive; any point within the histogram can be clicked and the corresponding observations will be highlighted in the data table (Figure 9.4). By default, menus are hidden from view; hovering the arrow over the thin gray bar or pressing the 'Alt' key will make the menu appear. The auto-hiding option can be turned off by altering the preferences: File > preferences > windows specific and select your preferences for auto-hide menu and toolbars.

BUILDING FREQUENCY TABLES AND GRAPHICS

Next let's look a little closer at our data using a JMP platform, TABULATE. To begin, hover over the gray bar above distribution to view the menu, then

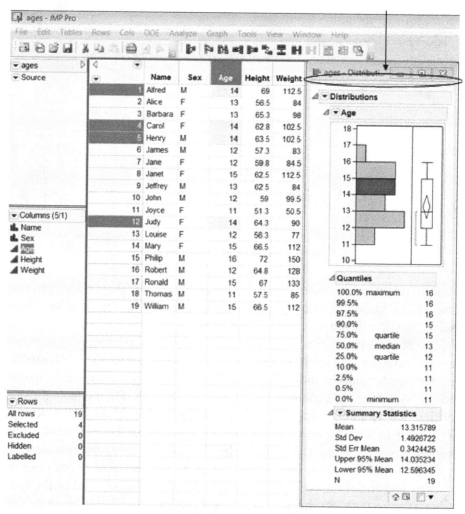

FIGURE 9.4. Distributions in JMP.

select the tables menu and click tabulate. Within TABULATE, tables can be customized using available control panel options such as N, Column %, Row %, and % of Total. By single-clicking variables and/or statistics and then dragging and dropping into columns or rows (Figure 9.5), frequency tables like those seen in Figure 6.3. can be created.

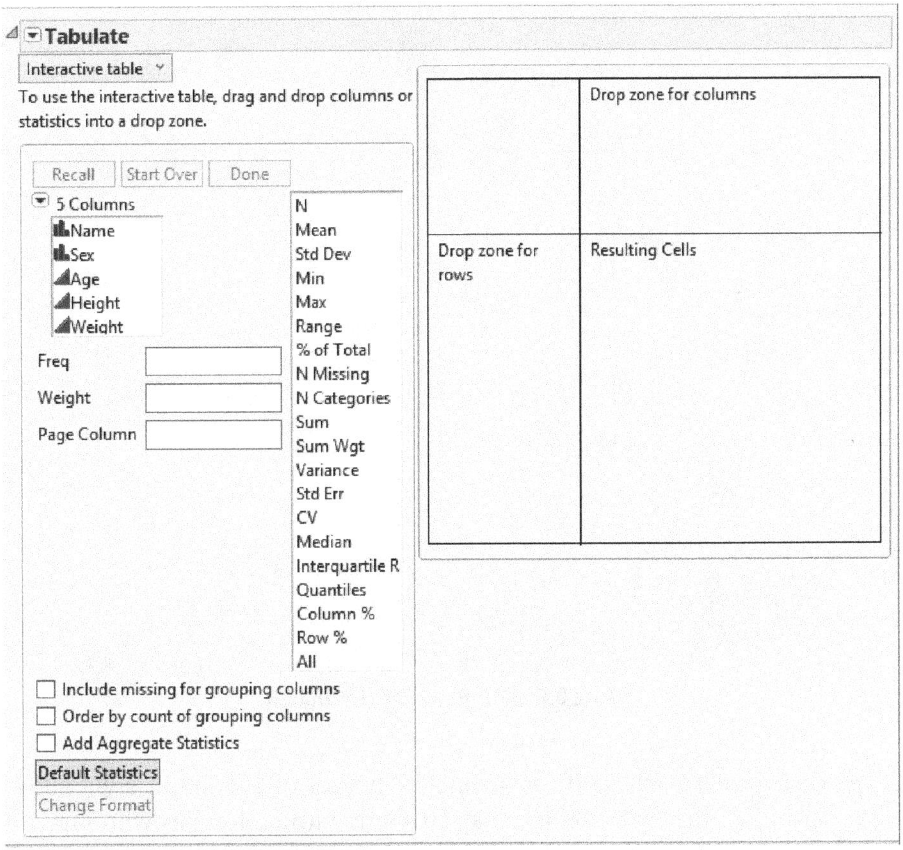

FIGURE 9.5. TABULATE Window in JMP Pro.

The JMP GRAPH BUILDER operates similarly to TABULATE, allowing the user to drag and drop variables in order to create customized graphics. Begin by activating the toolbar and selecting graph > graph builder. In this example, the variable Weight will be placed on the X axis, Height on the Y axis, and Sex, used to stratify the data, placed in the horizontal space on top labeled "group X." Icons for each available graph type are located along the top; graph types can be changed by clicking on these icons. Different types of charts include histograms, boxplots, maps, contour plots, and several more. While creating visually appealing graphical displays is frequently straightforward, determining which display is most representative of the data is often more complex.

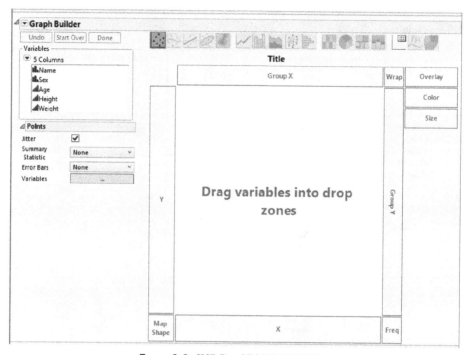

FIGURE 9.6. JMP Pro GRAPH BUILDER.

Hovering over each icon for a quick synopsis of the graph style allows the user to test-drive all the options. To share with colleagues who may not have access to JMP, the graphic can be saved to alternative file extensions. Figure 9.6 was saved as an .rtf file for easy access in Microsoft Word. For a more in-depth discussion of the possibilities in JMP GRAPH BUILDER, go to http://www.jmp.com/en_us/support.html.

IMPORTING DATA USING JMP

For SAS programmers who prefer not to write their own syntax for importing data or who are importing data with an unusual format JMP can be a great alternative to traditional methods in SAS. The software easily imports various file types, including Excel, text, HTML, and SAS. In Chapter 1 we discussed using the SAS import wizard as an alternative to writing syntax; however, data can come in formats that are not supported by the wizard, and for that JMP offers ultimate flexibility. The 'DATA WITH PREVIEW' option for opening

Graph Builder

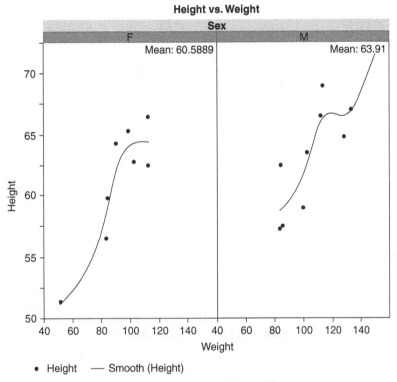

FIGURE 9.7. 'Smoother' Graph in .rtf Format.

a data table is a convenient method when data needs to be previewed and possibly manipulated even prior to import. Using this technique, the user can manually move columns and indicate delimiters and headings.

In Figure 9.8, a Microsoft Excel file is opened in JMP with this option; notice that we can easily indicate at which line column names are located, the line on which data starts, and the indicator for the end of a field. Once we are satisfied with the imported data as a JMP data table, the data can be explored here or it can be saved as a SAS dataset (Figure 9.9).

JMP software is visual, interactive, and can help import files of various formats. The user can create tables, explore and manipulate variables, and save data as SAS datasets for easy use in programming. JMP graphics can be saved in a variety of formats and to make electronic sharing a breeze. In JMP, the programmer can see deeply into the data with just a few mouse clicks.

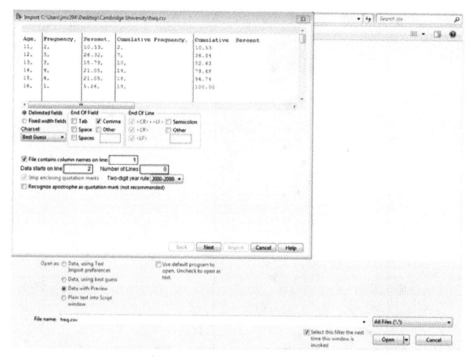

FIGURE 9.8 Importing Data with JMP.

File name:	Spring.jmp
Save as type:	JMP Data Table (*.jmp)
	JMP Data Table (*.jmp)
	Excel Workbook (*.xlsx;*.xls)
	Text Export File (*.txt)
	SAS Data Set (*.sas7bdat)
	SAS Transport File (*.xpt)

FIGURE 9.9. Saving a JMP Dataset.

TEST YOUR SKILLS

Using the sashelp dataset 'shoes' and the information presented in this chapter, accomplish the following tasks.

9.1 Open the SAS dataset 'Shoes' as a JMP data table.

9.2 Look at the distributions of the variables 'Sales', 'Inventory', and 'Returns'.

9.3 What is the data type of the variable 'Product'?

9.4 Using the graph builder, determine which types of shoes have the highest rate of return.

SOLUTIONS

9.1 Open the SAS dataset 'Shoes' as a JMP data table.
Save the dataset to your desktop:

```
libname x 'Desktop';
data x.shoes;
set sashelp.shoes;
run;
```

Open JMP, go to the File menu, choose open, and select the file saved to your desktop.

9.2 Look at the distributions of the variables 'Sales', 'Inventory', and 'Returns'. On the toolbar click Analyze > Distribution drag the variables 'sales', 'inventory', and 'returns' to the Y, Columns box, then click OK.

9.3 What is the data type of the variable 'Product'?
Data Type = Character

9.4 Using the graph builder, determine which types of shoes have the highest rate of return.

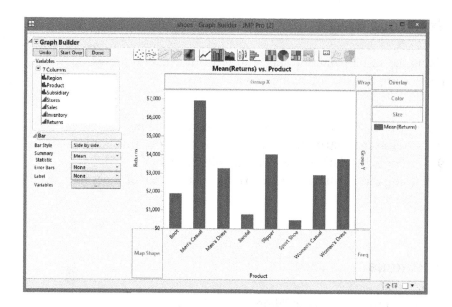

Index